ANNOUNCING ⌐
NOW REA

MW01257690

The edition of *The Complete Works of Frances Ridley Havergal* has five parts.

Volume I *Behold Your King:*
The Complete Poetical Works of Frances Ridley Havergal

Volume II *Whose I Am and Whom I Serve:*
Prose Works of Frances Ridley Havergal

Volume III *Loving Messages for the Little Ones:*
Works for Children by Frances Ridley Havergal

Volume IV *Love for Love: Frances Ridley Havergal:*
Memorials, Letters and Biographical Works

Volume V *Songs of Truth and Love:*
Music by Frances Ridley Havergal and William Henry Havergal

David L. Chalkley, Editor   Dr. Glen T. Wegge, Music Editor

The Music of Frances Ridley Havergal by Glen T. Wegge, Ph.D.

This Companion Volume to the Havergal edition is a valuable presentation of F.R.H.'s extant scores. Except for a very few of her hymntunes published in hymnbooks, most or nearly all of F.R.H.'s scores have been very little—if any at all—seen, or even known of, for nearly a century. What a valuable body of music has been unknown for so long and is now made available to many. Dr. Wegge completed his Ph.D. in Music Theory at Indiana University at Bloomington, and his diligence and thoroughness in this volume are obvious. First an analysis of F.R.H.'s compositions is given, an essay that both addresses the most advanced musicians and also reaches those who are untrained in music; then all the extant scores that have been found are newly typeset, with complete texts for each score and extensive indices at the end of the book. This volume presents F.R.H.'s music in newly typeset scores diligently prepared by Dr. Wegge, and Volume V of the Havergal edition presents the scores in facsimile, the original 19th century scores. (The essay—a dissertation—analysing her scores is given the same both in this Companion Volume and in Volume V of the Havergal edition.)

Dr. Wegge is also preparing all of these scores for publication in performance folio editions.

An undated photograph of F.R.H.

The Ministry

of Song.

BY

Frances Ridley Havergal

Taken from the New Edition of

The Complete Works of Frances Ridley Havergal

" Knowing her intense desire that Christ should be magnified, whether
by her life or in her death, may it be to His glory
that in these pages she, being dead,
' Yet speaketh ! ' "

THE MINISTRY OF SONG
Copyright © 2016 by
The Havergal Trust

ISBN 978-1-937236-51-9   Library of Congress: 2016918252

Cover Design by Glen T. Wegge.

Havergal, Frances Ridley
The Ministry of Song taken from the edition of the complete works of Frances
Ridley Havergal / Frances Ridley Havergal.

1. Havergal, Frances Ridley, 1836–1879. 2. Christian Life. 3. Christian Poetry,
English. 4. Music. I. Title

Printed in the United States of America.

This book is printed on acid-free paper.

This is taken from the new edition of *The Complete Works of Frances Ridley
Havergal* edited by David L. Chalkley, and Dr. Glen T. Wegge, Music Editor.

In all that she did, and in all that she wrote, Frances Ridley Havergal's one over-
riding desire was—as Colossians 1:18 says—"that in all things he [*her Lord*]
might have the pre-eminence." She saw herself as an instrument in her Sav-
iour's hand, writing for His sake, His glory alone. Indeed the words of Psalm
45:1 were true of her: "My heart is inditing a good matter: I speak of the things
which I have made touching the King: my tongue is the pen of a ready writer."

The truth of Christ, which she so loved, and which He used her to present
to others, is what is relevant and important, not Frances herself. Understanding
the truth of this, you don't first of all think "what a wonderful, fine lady she was"
but "what a Saviour ! she had." Jesus Christ alone was changing her from what
she was, to become daily more like Himself. Frances would not want anyone to
look solely or primarily at her, but she would want all to see her Lord and Sav-
iour. He was her only beauty, righteousness, wisdom, her all. So as you embark
on reading, may you too see the Lord Jesus Christ. To see her King is what she
would have wanted, the true conclusion of her works and life, and of any genu-
ine disciple's works and life. What a Saviour! The Lamb is all the glory in Em-
manuel's land, the kingdom of God.

CONTENTS.

LIST OF ILLUSTRATIONS

" WHAT I DO, THOU KNOWEST NOT NOW, BUT THOU SHALT KNOW HEREAFTER."

We shall know why the Cross was so hard
    to bear,
In the day when the Crowns are won ;
Why the " marching time " was so long
    and sore,
In the Land where the march is done !

We shall know why the Master came in
    the night,
And called us to follow Him ;
Up the blood-stained Way, amid storm
    and blast,
Where the shadows were long and dim !

We shall know why the Lord oft hid His Face,
And left us so sad and lone ;
In the Land, where the soul will in
    rapture gaze,
On the Blessed Three in One !

We shall know, why our streams of
    earthly joy,
So often ceased their flow ;
In the Land, where the River of Life
    rolls on,
'Neath the beams of the " *Emerald Bow !*"

We shall know why the Shepherd leads
    His flock,
O'er a barren and lonely way ;
In the Land, where the " *shadows*" can
    fall no more,
In the Land of Unclouded Day !

Harriet Kinnaway.

This poem by Harriet Kinnaway was found among Havergal manuscripts and papers. See F.R.H.'s poem "Not Yet" on pages 16–17 of this book.

The PERFECT SATISFACTION with which a HOLY GOD regards the PERFECT WORK of His Beloved SON, is the ground of a believing Sinner's PERFECT PEACE.

Edinburgh : James Taylor, 81 Castle Street.

This small card was found among Havergal manuscripts and papers. Who wrote this is not known. Colossians 2:10 Such cards and leaflets were and are easy and inexpensive to print, a means of God to give rich truths to many people, both friends and strangers. F.R.H.'s sister, Ellen Prestage Shaw, quoted this in a letter to her son Alfred Havergal Shaw (on page 758 of Volume IV of the Havergal edition, left column, lines 5–8).

This was F.R.H.'s personal seal.

The Ministry of Song.

A sterling volume of poems, *The Ministry of Song* was Frances Ridley Havergal's first published book. First published in 1869 by the Christian Book Society, 22 King William Street, Strand, London, this was taken up and published in 1871 by James Nisbet & Co., her primary publisher while she lived and after she died. We have extant two poems by F.R.H. (December 14,1836 to June 3, 1879) written in 1849 when she was twelve, and likely she had written others before those. *The Ministry of Song* was first published when she was thirty-two, the inscription on the dedication page said "To my Father." After Rev. William Henry Havergal (January 18, 1793 to April 19, 1870) died, the inscription in the first Nisbet edition was changed to be "To my Father's Memory."

Like her father, Frances was a remarkably gifted musician, the finest sort, and her poetry is very musical, exceptionally and finely so, true music through words without notes, full of rhythms and cadences and musical aspects. Note that this first book published by her was a collection of poems entitled *The Ministry of Song* (no notes nor staves, full of music), and her 1878 volume of poetry *Loyal Responses* (also words only, full of music) had the sub-title "Daily Melodies for the King's Minstrels." There are many examples of her poems that exemplify music in the words. Poetry is the part of language closest to music, at the edge or border where language and music meet, and Frances' poetry reflects her deep, profound musicianship. Just as Havergal's poem "Seulement pour Toi" ("Only for Thee," written on July 23, 1876 and posthumously published in *Under His Shadow* in 1879) needs (requires) a person with an advanced knowledge of French to see the beauty and power of that French poem, similarly a true musician can see rich details in the warp and woof of Frances' poetry and other works which are very reflective of a true musician, which others who are not musicians might easily miss. Apart from her performance and compositions, which were so valuable for those who heard her, she was a musician to the core, and her musical gifts enrich her other works, her poetry and prose.

Her works, both poetry and prose, are notably consistent in the fineness of both the ideas and the presentation of the ideas. The content of the ideas is more important than the presentation of the ideas, though both content and presentation are so very important.

There is a special beauty in her poetry (and also in her prose and in her music scores), true art and true beauty, both in her presentation of the ideas and in the content of the ideas. There is such rich truth presented in her poems. Numerous examples of this could be given, but "Just when Thou wilt" (pages 556–557 of Volume I of the Havergal edition) and "The Song of a Summer

Stream" (pages 163–164 of Volume I) are two suggested examples to read now.

In a letter to her friend—and a fine poet—Julia Kirchhoffer, on April 9, 1876, Frances wrote this about poetry:

I have an idea that metre answers to key in music, and that one may introduce modulation of metre exactly as one introduces modulation of key, and with similar mental effect. I have tried it in several recent longish poems, using different metres for different parts, and modulating from one into the other instead of passing directly. You will see what I mean in "The Sowers," where, instead of jumping direct into the rather jubilant metre of the last part, I work up to it through "One by one no longer," etc.[1]

Another example is a phrase that she wrote in another (earlier, likely 1874) letter, "musical thoughts," when she was referring not to composing music but to writing poetry. [2]

In the research on the edition of *The Complete Works of Frances Ridley Havergal*, a copy of *The Ministry of Song* was found with this printing number and address on the title page: 151st Thousand, James Nisbet & Co., 21 Berners Street, London (likely printed before 1906). O, that many in our day would see the true value in this book that is described in these next reviews published in her lifetime.

David L. Chalkley and Dr. Glen T. Wegge, November, 2016

[1] *Memorials of Frances Ridley Havergal* by Maria V. G. Havergal, page 197 of the original book, page 53 of Volume IV of *The Complete Works of Frances Ridley Havergal*. "The Sowers" is found on pages 407–418 of Volume I of the Havergal edition.

[2] *Memorials*, page 136 of the original book, page 38 of Volume IV of the Havergal edition. Here is the complete paragraph from that letter (likely written in 1874): "Dear Mr . W——, I can't make you quite understand me! You say 'F. R. H. could do "Satisfied" grandly'! No, she couldn't! Not unless He gave it me line by line! That is how verses come. The Master has not put a chest of poetic gold into my possession and said 'Now use it as you like!' But He keeps the gold, and gives it me piece by piece just when He will and as much as He will, and no more. Some day perhaps He will send me a bright line of verse on 'Satisfied' ringing through my mind, and then I shall look up and thank Him, and say, 'Now, dear Master, give me another to rhyme with it, and then another'; and then perhaps He will send it all in one flow of musical thoughts, but more likely one at a time, that I may be kept asking Him for every line. There, that is the process, and you see there is no 'I can do it' at all. That isn't His way with me. I often smile to myself when people talk about 'gifted pen' or 'clever verses,' etc.; because they don't know that it is neither, but something really much nicer than being 'talented' or 'clever.' "

The harp was F.R.H.'s personal emblem. This harp copied here was published on the front cover of her first book, The Ministry of Song *(published in 1869 by the Christian Book Society, London). She was a musician to the core.*

These next seven reviews (or excerpts of reviews) of *The Ministry of Song* (published in periodicals in the first two years before Nisbet took up this book) were found in an advertisement page at the back of *Pleasant Fruits* by Maria V. G. Havergal (1871, James Nisbet & Co.), with attribution to the original publisher, the Christian Book Society of London.

Second Edition, Crown 8vo, 5s., cloth.

THE
MINISTRY OF SONG.

"Genuine poetry. Many a bowed-down heart can in its pages be reminded of the way of peace, and of Him who can alone give that peace which the world cannot give, and in a way which is not the world's way."—*Press and St. James's Chronicle.*

"These sacred poems possess the rare and invaluable combination of religion, genius, and art. They are no mere rhymes, but the masterly renderings of a poet, a seer, a deep thinker."—*Morning Journal.*

"Rich in thought, sweet in experience, and most scriptural in doctrine."—*Gospel Magazine.*

"Critical nicety and power of phrase, variety of treatment, wealth and naturalness, lucid exposition. The grace, tenderness, purity, and devotional spirit of Miss Havergal's volume will make it warmly welcomed wherever Christian song and Christian sentiment are loved and appreciated."
—*Morning Advertiser.*

"Peculiarly pleasant, swallow-like flights. All her poems show much native truth, delicacy, and sweetness. We mention, as being especially fine, 'Three-fold Praise,' 'On the Last Leaf,' and 'Making Poetry.'"
—*Contemporary Review.*

"Those who wish for a summer-like breath of song, which shall be accordant with woods and waves, and the harmonies of the world that is, and the world that is to be, may do worse than appoint this fair minister of song to be their private chaplain."—*Edinburgh Daily Review.*

"Pure and elevating thoughts, pleasant fancy, and musical verse; remarkable for originality of thought as well as for graceful treatment."
—*Literary World.*

"The Ministry of Song will be a ministry for good to many a mind, and for many a year to come."—*Record.*

CHRISTIAN BOOK SOCIETY,
22 King William Street, London.

Next are five other reviews (or excerpts of published reviews) of this book, found in the advertisement pages at the back of an 1876 Nisbet copy of another book of poetry by F.R.H., *Under the Surface.*

Seventh Edition, royal 32mo, 1s. 6d. cloth, gilt.
THE MINISTRY OF SONG.

"A true poet, very rich in thought, and very musical in expression. Her book is vigorous as well as varied in imagery and pictorial power; . . . the tone always elevated and devout."—*Literary Times.*

"Rich in lovely thoughts most musically rendered; deep pathos, and heart knowledge. We hope this volume will be followed by many others."—*Bell's Messenger.*

"Poetical imagination, high intellectual attainment, intense earnestness of heart and purpose, and a remarkable power of melodious expression, present a rare combination. . . . Every poem is a gem; and every gem gathers lustre from its close proximity to the Pearl of Great Price. Her gems of song have become heart treasures."—*Our Own Fireside.*

"These poems bear witness that they have welled up from a heart which has learned, and listened, and suffered, before attempting to teach, or preach, or sing. She has learned of the Holy Spirit, and she sings of Jesus."—*The Christian.*

"The 'Ministry of Song' will be a ministry for good to many a mind, and for many a year to come."—*Record.*

176   *The Ministry of Song.*

Adoration.

O MASTER, at Thy feet
I bow in rapture sweet;
Before me, as in darkling glass,
Some glorious outlines pass,
Of love, and truth, and holiness, and power;
I own them Thine, O Christ, and bless Thee for this
     hour.

O full of truth and grace,
Smile of Jehovah's face,
O tenderest heart of love untold!
Who may Thy praise unfold?
Thee, Saviour, Lord of lords and King of kings,
Well may adoring seraphs hymn with veiling wings.

I have no words to bring
Worthy of Thee, my King,
And yet one anthem in Thy praise
I long, I long to raise;
The heart is full, the eye entranced above,
But words all melt away in silent awe and love.

How can the lip be dumb,
The hand all still and numb,
When Thee the heart doth see and own
Her Lord and God alone?
Tune for Thyself the music of my days,
And open Thou my lips that I may show Thy praise.

F.R.H.'s handwritten note next to "Adoration" in her personal copy of The Ministry of Song. *This was a special copy, with a blank page next to every printed page of the book.*

Adoration. 177

Yea, let my whole life be
One anthem unto Thee,
And let the praise of lip and life
Out-ring all sin and strife.
O Jesus, Master! be Thy name supreme
For heaven and earth the one, the grand, the eternal
theme.

NORWICH: FLETCHER AND SON, PRINTERS.

F.R.H.'s Hand-written Notes in Her Personal Copy of *The Ministry of Song*

Frances Ridley Havergal had a specially bound personal copy of her first published volume, *The Ministry of Song*. The title page says "Second Edition" and "London: Christian Book Society, 22 King William Street, Strand." On the inscription page are written only these words: "To My Father." This book was first published in 1869, inscribed to her father, Rev. William Henry Havergal. The later copies published by James Nisbet & Co. have on the inscription page "To my Father's Memory", published after his death April 19, 1870. This special copy had alternating sheets of printed text and blank sheets, so that across from every right-side page of printed text was a left-side blank page, and turning over the page, every left-side page of printed text faced a right-side blank page. Frances wrote notes on several of the poems in the volume, most of the notes being on the blank pages facing the poems, with a few notes at the top or bottom of poems on printed pages. Her handwriting here was beautiful and for the most part—with exceptions—readily legible.

    In the transcription of the notes, diligent effort was made to copy closely what she wrote. Comments not written by her are placed within brackets.

    [This note was written across from the beginning of "Prelude."]

This Prelude is verses 1 and 3 of an answer to a remark of A.J.S. in a letter to Maria. She had sent him 3 or 4 poems, asking him to criticize them. He replied, "Criticize a star, a rainbow, a fountain, but not Miss F. R. H.'s verses!" The answer commmenced,
    "No, not a <u>star</u>! That is a name too beautiful and bright
    For any earthly lay to wear in this our lingering sight,"
    But 'mid the broken waters etc."
Quoted in *Derbyshire Times*.
Mentioned in *Paisley Gazette*.

[At the bottom of the "Prelude" she wrote:] Dec<u>r</u> 26. 1859.

    [This note was written beneath the end of the poem "The Ministry of Song."]

Feb. 27. 1867.

Had in type from Strattam [or Shattam?], but his delay clashed with publication of Golden Sheaf, so I was in honour bound to the S. of this, and he withdrew it.

In D.O.T. for Janr 1868.

Quoted in *Bell's Messenger*, *Worcester Journal*, *Hereford Journal*, *Paisley Gazette*.

Appeared in *Worcester Herald*, Sept. 1869.

[This note was written at the end of "Threefold Praise."]

Febr 26. 1867.

Mentioned as "especially fine" in *Contemporary Review*.

Mentioned in *Derbyshire Times*.

Quotation from "Mendelssohn" in *Literary World*.

[This note was written across from the beginning of "One Question, Many Answers."]

I began writing this on my way to Germany in May /57 with Auguste [first name uncertain] Bender and August Fournier [last name uncertain]. A.B. saw me scribbling in a corner of the deck (going to Rotterdam) and I heard her remark to A.F. " . . . "! [5 words in German, illegible]

[This note was written at the end of "Sunbeams in the Wood."]

July 12. 1859.

Inserted in *Glasgow Morning Journal*.

Quoted in *Literary World*.

Mentioned in *Paisley Gazette*.

[In "Treasure Trove," the book had in the third line of the fourth stanza "treasure", to which Frances wrote this correction.]

? treasure<u>s</u>

[Later the Nisbet editions correctly printed "treasures."]

[This note was written across from the end of "Christ's Recall."]

Poor Carrie Lea chose this to be written in her book.

[This refers to the common practices of friends and acquaintances writing a greeting or quotation in a person's Album.]

[This note was written across from the beginning of "God the Provider."]

Extract from a letter to Mr. J. Parlane from the widow of a Scotch evangelist. "When you sent this account, it came the day after my beloved husband died. You enclosed a leaflet: the text at the heading was "My God shall supply all your need" and the last line of each verse was "God shall all your need supply." I cannot tell you the blessing I got in reading it, and each day it has been in my mind and I have felt its sweetness. And now your returning the money is another token of His faithfulness.

. . . _____ . . Mary Matheson.

Written at Bonn, June, 1866, for Mamma. ["Mamma" was her stepmother, Caroline Anne (Cook) Havergal.]

[This note was written across from the beginning of "This Same Jesus."]

Founded on a recollection of one sentence in a sermon of Papa's at St. N. [Saint Nicholas Church, Worcester] Nov. /56, which struck me more vividly and happily than almost anything I ever heard. I forget the words, but shall never forget the impression, nor the thrill which went through me as he said " . . . . . it will be 'this same Jesus.'" I'd developed a much earlier impression of the same kind,

1851. "This same Jesus" is one of the chief watchwords of my faith. I constantly recur to it, and I think it will be my comfort in the dark valley.

[This note was written below the ending of "This Same Jesus."]

Dec.11. 1864.
Quoted in *Literary World*—the whole.

Written at Oakh. [Oakhampton] on a Sunday at home from a shjwh [illegible word] accident. Given to U. L. C. The only piece that broke my 5 years silence—1860 to 1865.

[This note was written across from the beginning of "Daily Strength."]

The New Years Bells were ringing. I was sleeping with Maria, she roused me to hear them, and quoted the text "As thy day" etc. as a new year's motto. I did not answer, but presently returned it to her in rhyme (the two first verses, I think.) She was pleased, so I finished it next day, and gave it to her.
The last verse with a slight alteration was placed by my cousins on Aunt Izard's tomb—1868.
"Now thy days on earth are past,
Christ hath called, etc."

[Now thy days on earth are past,
Christ hath called thee home at last,
His redeeming love to praise,
Who hath strengthened all thy days.]

[This note was written at the bottom of "Daily Strength."]

Jan. 1. 1859.
Sunday Magazine July 1867.
Mentioned in *Paisley Gazette*.

[This note was written across from the beginning of "Master, Say On."]

Written at Weston, May /67.

[This note was written across from the beginning of "On the Last Leaf."]

Written at Oakhampton, Oct. /65.

[This note was written across from the beginning of "Making Poetry."]

Suggested by a nice little girl, Charlotte Thirler [last name illegible], who was spending her holidays at Abergele when I was there for a month in 1863. She made some really pretty little quatrains, and repeated one about a daisy to me "sitting on the window seat." She called it "making poetry", as children always do.

[This note was written at the end of "My Name."]

April 1. /68.

Mentioned in *Derbyshire Times*.
Quoted as "fiercely evangelical castigation to "cruel changeless Rome, in *Literary World*." [The quotation marks copy her handwritten note.]

[This note was written across from "Adoration." The note takes a page and a half in her handwriting, by far the longest one among these notes.]

I felt that I had not written any thing specially in praise to Christ—a strong longing to do so possessed me, I wanted to show for <u>His</u> praise, to <u>Him</u>, not to others—even if no mortal ever saw it. He would see every line, would know the unwritten longing to praise Him even if words failed utterly. It describes, as most of my poems do, rather reminiscence than present feeling.—I cannot transcribe at the moment of strong feeling [.] I <u>recall</u> it afterwards and write it down. "O <u>Master</u>"! It is perhaps my favourite title because it implies <u>sale</u>

and submission, and this is what love craves. Men may feel differently, but a true woman's submission is inseparable from deep love. I wrote it in the cold and twilight in the little back room, uncarpeted, at Shareshill Parsonage. Next morning, New Years Day, I was transcribing it after breakfast, and had just copied verse 4—when post brought me a note from Emily Bodington and a card.

> "Oh let my life, Great God, breathe forth
> A constant melody,
> And every action be a note
> In the sweet hymn to Thee."

I began my book with the expression of its devotion to God's glory. I wished to close it with a distinctive ascription of praise to <u>Jesus</u>, and therefore without any hesitation at once decided upon placing "Adoration" where it stands.

[The note above was written on the 2 blank pages across from the 2 printed pages of "Adoration."]

[The following note was written below the end of "Adoration."]

Dec. 31. 1866.
Inserted in *Sunday Magazine* Sept 1867.
Mentioned in *Glasgow Morning Journal* and had two last verses quoted in the *Paisley Gazette.*

[These were all the notes she wrote in the book.]

THE MINISTRY OF SONG.

To my Father's Memory.

Frances Ridley Havergal's first published book was *The Ministry of Song*, published in 1869 by the Christian Book Society of London. Her original inscription was "To My Father." Her father, Rev. William Henry Havergal, died in 1870, and the inscription "To my Father's Memory." was placed at the front of the book when James Nisbet & Co. published *The Ministry of Song* in 1871. This is a facsimile copy of the inscription in this place in Nisbet's *The Poetical Works of Frances Ridley Havergal*.

The Ministry of Song.

Prelude.

AMID the broken waters of our ever-restless thought,
Oh be my verse an answering gleam from higher radiance caught;
That where through dark o'erarching boughs of sorrow, doubt, and sin,
The glorious Star of Bethlehem upon the flood looks in,
Its tiny trembling ray may bid some downcast vision turn
To that enkindling Light, for which all earthly shadows yearn.
Oh be my verse a hidden stream, which silently may flow
Where drooping leaf and thirsty flower in lonely valleys grow;
And often by its shady course to pilgrim hearts be brought
The quiet and refreshment of an upward-pointing thought;
Till, blending with the broad bright stream of sanctified endeavour,
God's glory be its ocean home, the end it seeketh ever.

The Ministry of Song.

IN God's great field of labour
    All work is not the same;
He hath a service for each one
    Who loves His holy name.
And you, to whom the secrets
    Of all sweet sounds are known,
Rise up! for He hath called you
    To a mission of your own.
And, rightly to fulfil it,
    His grace can make you strong,
Who to your charge hath given
    The Ministry of Song.

Sing to the little children,
    And they will listen well;
Sing grand and holy music,
    For they can feel its spell.

3

Tell them the tale of Jephthah;
    Then sing them what he said,—
'Deeper and deeper still,' and watch
    How the little cheek grows red,
And the little breath comes quicker:
    They will ne'er forget the tale,
Which the song has fastened surely,
    As with a golden nail.

I remember, late one evening,
    How the music stopped, for, hark!
Charlie's nursery door was open,
    He was calling in the dark,—
'Oh no! I am not frightened,
    And I do not want a light;
But I cannot sleep for thinking
    Of the song you sang last night.
Something about a "valley,"
    And "make rough places plain,"
And "Comfort ye;" so beautiful!
    Oh, sing it me again!'

Sing at the cottage bedside;
    They have no music there,
And the voice of praise is silent
    After the voice of prayer.
Sing of the gentle Saviour
    In the simplest hymns you know,
And the pain-dimmed eye will brighten
    As the soothing verses flow.
Better than loudest plaudits
    The murmured thanks of such,
For the King will stoop to crown them
    With His gracious 'Inasmuch.'

Sing, where the full-toned organ
    Resounds through aisle and nave,
And the choral praise ascendeth
    In concord sweet and grave.
Sing, where the village voices
    Fall harshly on your ear;

And, while more earnestly you join,
 Less discord you will hear.
The noblest and the humblest
 Alike are 'common praise,'
And not for human ear alone
 The psalm and hymn we raise.

Sing in the deepening twilight,
 When the shadow of eve is nigh,
And her purple and golden pinions
 Fold o'er the western sky.
Sing in the silver silence,
 While the first moonbeams fall;
So shall your power be greater
 Over the hearts of all.
Sing till you bear them with you
 Into a holy calm,
And the sacred tones have scattered
 Manna, and myrrh, and balm.

Sing! that your song may gladden;
 Sing like the happy rills,
Leaping in sparkling blessing
 Fresh from the breezy hills.
Sing! that your song may silence
 The folly and the jest,
And the 'idle word' be banished
 As an unwelcome guest.
Sing! that your song may echo
 After the strain is past,
A link of the love-wrought cable
 That holds some vessel fast.

Sing to the tired and anxious
 It is yours to fling a ray,
Passing indeed, but cheering,
 Across the rugged way.
Sing to God's holy servants,
 Weary with loving toil,
Spent with their faithful labour
 On oft ungrateful soil.

The chalice of your music
 All reverently bear,
For with the blessèd angels
 Such ministry you share.

When you long to bear the Message
 Home to some troubled breast,
Then sing with loving fervour,
 'Come unto Him, and rest.'
Or would you whisper comfort,
 Where words bring no relief,
Sing how 'He was despisèd,
 Acquainted with our grief.'
And, aided by His blessing,
 The song may win its way
Where speech had no admittance,
 And change the night to day.

Sing, when His mighty mercies
 And marvellous love you feel,
And the deep joy of gratitude
 Springs freshly as you kneel;
When words, like morning starlight,
 Melt powerless,—rise and sing!
And bring your sweetest music
 To Him your gracious King.
Pour out your song before Him
 To whom our best is due;
Remember, He who hears your prayer
 Will hear your praises too.

Sing on in grateful gladness!
 Rejoice in this good thing
Which the Lord thy God hath given thee,
 The happy power to sing.
But yield to Him, the Sovereign,
 To whom all gifts belong,
In fullest consecration,
 Your Ministry of Song,

Until His mercy grant you
   That resurrection voice,
Whose only ministry shall be,
   To praise Him and rejoice.

Our Hidden Leaves.

OH the hidden leaves of Life!
   Closely folded in the heart;
Leaves where Memory's golden finger,
Slowly pointing, loves to linger;
   Leaves that bid the old tears start.

Leaves where Hope would read the future,
   Sibylline, and charged with fate:
Leaves which calm Submission closeth,
While her tearless eye reposeth
   On the legend, 'Trust, and wait!'

Leaves which grave Experience ponders,
   Soundings for her pilot-charts;
Leaves which God Himself is storing,
Records which we read, adoring
   Him who writes on human hearts.

All our own, our treasured secrets,
   Indestructible archives!
None can copy, none can steal them,
Death itself shall not reveal them,
   Sacred manuscripts of lives.

Some are filled with fairy pictures,
   Half imagined and half seen;
Radiant faces, fretted towers,
Sunset colours, starry flowers,
   Wondrous arabesques between.

Some are traced with liquid sunbeams,
    Some with fire, and some with tears;
Some with crimson dyes are glowing,
From a smitten life-rock flowing
    Through the wilderness of years.

Some are crossed with later writing,
    Palimpsests of earliest days;
Old remembrance faintly gleaming
Through the thinking and the dreaming
    Outlines dim in noontide haze.

One lies open, all unwritten,
    To the glance of careless sight;
Yet it bears a shining story,
Traced in phosphorescent glory,
    Only legible by night.

One is dark with hieroglyphics
    Of some dynasty of grief:
Only God, and just one other,
Dearest friend, or truest brother,
    Ever read that hidden leaf.

Many a leaf is undeciphered,
    Writ in languages unknown;
O'er the strange inscription bending,
(Every clue in darkness ending,)
    Finding no 'Rosetta Stone,'

Still we study, always failing!
    God can read it, we must wait;
Wait, until He teach the mystery,
Then the wisdom-woven history
    Faith shall read, and Love translate.

Leaflets now unpaged and scattered
    Time's great library receives;
When eternity shall bind them,
Golden volumes we shall find them,
    God's light falling on the leaves.

Threefold Praise.

HAYDN—MENDELSSOHN—HANDEL

'We bless Thee for our creation, preservation, and all the blessings of this life; but above all, for Thine inestimable love in the redemption of the world by our Lord Jesus Christ.'

PART I.

'We bless Thee for our creation.'

Haydn's 'Creation.'

WHAT is the first and simplest praise,
    The universal debt,
Which yet the thoughtless heart of man
    So quickly may forget?
'We bless Thee for creation!'
    So taught the noble band
Who left a sound and holy form,
    For ages yet to stand,
Rich legacy of praise and prayer,
    Laid up through ages past,
Strong witness for the truth of God:
    Oh, may we hold it fast!

'We bless Thee for creation!'
    So are we blithely taught
By Haydn's joyous spirit;
    Such was the praise he brought.
A praise all morning sunshine,
    And sparklers of the spring,
O'er which the long life-shadows
    No chastening softness fling.

A praise of early freshness,
    Of carol and of trill,
Re-echoing all the music
    Of valley and of rill.
A praise that we are sharing
    With every singing breeze,

With nightingales and linnets,
    With waterfalls and trees;
With anthems of the flowers
    Too delicate and sweet
For all their fairy minstrelsy
    Our mortal ears to greet.

A mighty song of blessing
    Archangels too uplift,
For their own bright existence,
    A grand and glorious gift.
But such their full life-chalice,
    So sparkling and so pure,
And such their vivid sense of joy
    Sweet, solid, and secure,
We cannot write the harmonies
    To such a song of bliss,
We only catch the melody,
    And sing, content with this.

We are but little children,
    And earth a broken toy;
We do not know the treasures
    In our Father's house of joy.
Thanksgivings for creation
    We ignorantly raise;
We know not yet the thousandth part
    Of that for which we praise.

Yet, praise Him for creation!
    Nor cease the happy song,
But this our Hallelujah
    Through all our life prolong;
'T will mingle with the chorus
    Before the heavenly throne,
Where what it truly is TO BE
    Shall first be fully known.

PART II.

'. . . preservation, and all the blessings of this life.'

Mendelssohn's 'Elijah.'

O FELIX! happy in thy varied store
Of harmonies undreamt before,
   How different was the gift
   Of praise 'twas thine to pour,
Whether in stately calm, or tempest strong and swift!

     Mark the day,
     In mourning robe of grey,
Of shrouded mountain and of storm-swept vale,
And purple pall spread o'er the distance pale,
   While thunderous masses wildly drift
In lurid gloom and grandeur: then a swift
And dazzling ray bursts through a sudden rift;
The dark waves glitter as the storms subside,
And all is light and glory at the eventide.

   O sunlight of thanksgiving! Who that knows
   Its bright forth-breaking after dreariest days,
     Would change the after-thought of woes
     For memory's loveliest light that glows,
If so he must forego one note of that sweet praise?

     For not the song
   Which knows no minor cadence, sad and long;
     And not the tide
     Whose emerald and silver pride
Was never dashed in wild and writhing fray,
Where grim and giant rocks hurl back the spray;
   And not the crystal atmosphere,
   That carves each outline sharp and clear
Upon a sapphire sky: not these, not these,
Nor aught existing but to charm and please,
Without acknowledging life's mystery,
     And all the mighty reign
     Of yearning and of pain
That fills its half-read history,

Fit music can supply
To lift the wandering heart on high
To that Preserving Love, which rules all change,
And gives 'all blessings of this life,' so dream-like and so strange.

And his was praise
Deeper and truer, such as those may raise
Who know both shade and sunlight, and whose life
Hath learnt victorious strife
Of courage and of trust and hope still dear,
With passion and with grief, with danger and with fear.

———————

Upriseth now a cry,
Plaintive and piercing, to the brazen sky:
Help, Lord! the harvest days are gone;
Help, Lord! for other help is none;
The infant children cry for bread,
And no man breaketh it. The suckling's tongue for thirst
Now cleaveth to his mouth. Our land is cursed;
Our wasted Zion mourns, in vain her hands are spread.

A mother's tale of grief,
Of sudden blight upon the chief,
The *only* flower of love that cheered her widowed need:
O loneliest! O desolate indeed!
Were it not mockery to whisper here
A word of hope and cheer?

A mountain brow, an awe-struck crowd,
The prayer-sent flame, the prayer-sent cloud,
A mighty faith, a more than kingly power,
Changed for depression's darkest hour,
For one lone shadow in the desert sought,
A fainting frame, a spirit overwrought,
A sense of labour vain, and strength all spent for nought.

Death hovering near,
With visible terror-spear
Of famine, or a murder-stainèd sword,

A stricken land forsaken of her Lord;
    While bowed with doubled fear,
    The faithful few appear;
O sorrows manifold outpoured!
Is blessing built upon such dark foundation;
And can a temple rising from such woe,
Rising upon such mournful crypts below,
Be filled with light and joy and sounding adoration?

O strange mosaic! wondrously inlaid
    Are all its depths of shade,
With beauteous stones of promise, marbles fair
Of trust and calm, and flashing brightly, there
The precious gems of praise are set, and shine
Resplendent with a light that almost seems Divine.

    Thanks be to God!
    The thirsty land He laveth,
    The perishing He saveth;
    The floods lift up their voices,
    The answering earth rejoices.
Thanks be to Him, and never-ending laud,
For this new token of His bounteous love,
Who reigns in might the waterfloods above:
    The gathering waters rush along;
And leaps the exultant shout, one cataract of song,
    Thanks be to God!

    Thus joyously we sing;
Nor is this all the praise we bring.
We need not wait for earthquake, storm, and fire
    To lift our praises higher;
Nor wait for heaven-dawn ere we join the hymn
    Of throne-surrounding cherubim;
For even on earth their anthem hath begun,
To Him, the Mighty and the Holy One.

We know the still small Voice in many a word
Of guidance, and command, and promise heard;
And, knowing it, we bow before His feet,

With love and awe the seraph-strain repeat,
Holy, Holy, Holy! God the Lord!
His glory fills the earth, His name be all-adored.

O Lord, our Lord! how excellent Thy name
Throughout this universal frame!
Therefore Thy children rest
Beneath the shadow of Thy wings,
A shelter safe and blest;
And tune their often tremulous strings
Thy love to praise, Thy glory to proclaim,
The Merciful, the Gracious One, eternally The Same.

PART III.

'. . . but above all, for Thine inestimable love in the redemption of the world by our Lord Jesus Christ.'

Handel's 'Messiah.'

HUSH! for a master harp is tuned again,
In truest unison with choirs above,
For prelude to a loftier, sweeter strain,
The praise of God's inestimable love;
Who sent redemption to a world of woe,
That all a Father's heart His banished ones might know.

Hush! while on silvery wing of holiest song
Floats forth the old, dear story of our peace,
His coming, the Desire of Ages long,
To wear our chains, and win our glad release.
Our wondering joy, to hear such tidings blest,
Is crowned with 'Come to Him, and He will give you rest.'

Rest, by His sorrow! Bruisèd for our sin,
Behold the Lamb of God! His death our life.
Now lift your heads, ye gates! He entereth in,
Christ risen indeed, and Conqueror in the strife.
Thanks, thanks to Him who won, and Him who gave
Such victory of love, such triumph o'er the grave.

Hark! 'Hallelujah!' O sublimest strain!
    Is it prophetic echo of the day
When He, our Saviour and our King, shall reign,
    And all the earth shall own His righteous sway?
Lift heart and voice, and swell the mighty chords,
While hallelujahs peal, to Him, the Lord of lords!

    'Worthy of all adoration,
       Is the Lamb that once was slain,'
    Cry, in raptured exultation,
    His redeemed from every nation;
       Angel myriads join the strain,
    Sounding from their sinless strings
    Glory to the King of kings:
    Harping, with their harps of gold,
    Praise which never can be told.

    Hallelujahs full and swelling
       Rise around His throne of might,
    All our highest laud excelling,
    Holy and immortal, dwelling
       In the unapproachèd light,
    He is worthy to receive
    All that heaven and earth can give;
    Blessing, honour, glory, might,
    All are His by glorious right.

    As the sound of many waters
       Let the full Amen arise!
    HALLELUJAH! Ceasing never,
    Sounding through the great FOR EVER,
       Linking all its harmonies;
    Through eternities of bliss,
    Lord, our rapture shall be this;
    And our endless life shall be
    One AMEN of praise to Thee.

Not Yet.

JOHN 13:7.

NOT yet thou knowest what I do,
    O feeble child of earth,
Whose life is but to angel view
    The morning of thy birth!
The smallest leaf, the simplest flower,
    The wild bee's honey-cell,
Have lessons of My love and power
    Too hard for thee to spell.

Thou knowest not how I uphold
    The little thou dost scan;
And how much less canst thou unfold
    My universal plan,
Where all thy mind can grasp of space
    Is but a grain of sand;—
The time thy boldest thought can trace,
    One ripple on the strand!

Not yet thou knowest what I do,
    In this wild, warring world,
Whose prince doth still triumphant view
    Confusion's flag unfurled;
Nor how each proud and daring thought
    Is subject to My will,
Each strong and secret purpose brought
    My counsel to fulfil.

Not yet thou knowest how I bid
    Each passing hour entwine
Its grief or joy, its hope or fear,
    In one great love-design;
Nor how I lead thee through the night,
    By many a various way,
Still upward to unclouded light,
    And onward to the day.

Not yet thou knowest what I do
    Within thine own weak breast,
To mould thee to My image true,
    And fit thee for My rest.
But yield thee to My loving skill;
    The veilèd work of grace,
From day to day progressing still,
    It is not thine to trace.

Yes, walk by faith and not by sight,
    Fast clinging to My hand;
Content to feel My love and might,
    Not yet to understand.
A little while thy course pursue,
    Till grace to glory grow;
Then what I am, and what I do,
    Hereafter thou shalt know.

Thanksgiving.

THANKS be to God! to whom earth owes
    Sunshine and breeze,
The heath-clad hill, the vale's repose,
    Streamlet and seas,
The snowdrop and the summer rose,
    The many-voicèd trees.

Thanks for the darkness that reveals
    Night's starry dower;
And for the sable cloud that heals
    Each fevered flower;
And for the rushing storm that peals
    Our weakness and Thy power.

Thanks for the sweetly-lingering might
    In music's tone;
For paths of knowledge, whose calm light
    Is all Thine own;
For thoughts that at the Infinite
    Fold their bright wings alone.

Yet thanks that silence oft may flow
In dewlike store;
Thanks for the mysteries that show
How small our lore;
Thanks that we here so little know,
And trust Thee all the more!

Thanks for the gladness that entwines
Our path below;
Each sunrise that incarnadines
The cold, still snow;
Thanks for the light of love which shines
With brightest earthly glow.

Thanks for the sickness and the grief
Which none may flee;
For loved ones standing now around
The crystal sea;
And for the weariness of heart
Which only rests in Thee.

Thanks for Thine own thrice-blessèd Word,
And Sabbath rest;
Thanks for the hope of glory stored
In mansions blest;
Thanks for the Spirit's comfort poured
Into the trembling breast.

Thanks, more than thanks, to Him ascend,
Who died to win
Our life, and every trophy rend
From Death and Sin;
Till, when the thanks of Earth shall end,
The thanks of Heaven begin.

NOTE.—It may be well to say, that these verses were in print before the writer either
saw or heard of the beautiful little poem by Adelaide Proctor on the same theme.

Life-Crystals.

THE world is full of crystals. Swift, or slow,
Or dark, or bright their varying formation;
From pure calm heights of fair untrodden snow
To fire-wrought depths of earliest creation.
And life is full of crystals; forming still
In myriad-shaped results from good and seeming ill.

Yes! forming everywhere; in busiest street,
In noisiest throng. Oh how it would astound us,
The strange soul-chemistry of some we meet
In slight and passing talk! For all around us,
Deep inner silence broods o'er gems to be.
Now, in three visioned hearts trace out the work with me!

A heart that wonderingly received the flow
Of marvels and of mysteries of being,
Of sympathies and tensions, joy and woe;
Each earnestly from baser substance freeing:
A great life-mixture, full, and deep, and strong:
A sudden touch, and lo! it crystallized in song.

Then forth it flashed among the souls of men
Its own prismatic radiance, brightly sealing
A several rainbow for each several ken;
The secrets of the distant stars revealing;
Reflecting many a heart's clear rays unknown,
And, freely shedding light, it analyzed their own.

A heart from which all joy had ebbed away,
And grief poured in a flood of burning anguish,
Then sealed the molten glow; till, day by day,
The fires without, within, begin to languish:
Then 'afterward' came coolness; all was well,
And from the broken crust a shining crystal fell.

A mourner found, and fastened on her breast
The soft-hued gem, the prized by mourners only;

With sense of treasure gained she sought her rest,
No longer wandering in the twilight lonely;
The sorrow-crystal glittering in the dark,
While faith and hope shone out to greet its starry spark.

A heart where emptiness seemed emptier made
By colourless remains of tasteless pleasure;
ONE came, and pitying the hollow shade,
Poured in His own strong love in fullest measure;
Then shadowed it with silent falling night,
And stilled it with the solemn Presence of His might.

A little while, then found the Master there
Love-crystals, sparkling in the joyous morning;
He stooped to gaze, and smiled to own them fair,
A treasured choice for His own rich adorning;
Then set them in His diadem above,
To mingle evermore with His own light and love.

Not Your Own.

'NOT your own!' but His ye are,
    Who hath paid a price untold
For your life, exceeding far
    All earth's store of gems and gold.
With the precious blood of Christ,
Ransom treasure all unpriced,
Full redemption is procured,
Full salvation is assured.

'Not your own!' but His by right,
    His peculiar treasure now,
Fair and precious in His sight,
    Purchased jewels for His brow.
He will keep what thus He sought,
Safely guard the dearly bought,
Cherish that which He did choose,
Always love and never lose.

'Not your own!' but His, the King,
　　His, the Lord of earth and sky,
His, to whom archangels bring
　　Homage deep and praises high.
What can royal birth bestow?
Or the proudest titles show?
Can such dignity be known
As the glorious name, 'His own!'

'Not your own!' To Him ye owe
　　All your life and all your love;
Live, that ye His praise may show,
　　Who is yet all praise above.
Every day and every hour,
Every gift and every power,
Consecrate to Him alone,
Who hath claimed you for His own.

Teach us, Master, how to give
　　All we have and are to Thee;
Grant us, Saviour, while we live,
　　Wholly, only, Thine to be.
Henceforth be our calling high
Thee to serve and glorify;
Ours no longer, but Thine own,
Thine for ever, Thine alone!

Wounded.

ONLY a look and a motion that nobody saw or heard,
Past in a moment and over, with never the sound of a word;
Streams of converse around me smoothly and cheerily flow,
But a terrible stab has been given, a silent and staggering blow.

Guesses the hand that gave it hardly a tithe of the smart,
Nothing at all of the anguish that fiercely leapt up in my heart,
Scorching and scathing its peace, while a tremulous nerve to the brain
Flashed up a telegram sudden, a message of quivering pain.

They must be merry without me, for how can I sing to-night?
They will only think I am tired, and thoughtfully shade the light;
Finger and voice would fail while the wound is open and sore;
Bleeding away the strength I had gathered for days before.

Only a look and a motion! Yes, but we little know
How from each dwarf-like 'only' a giant of power may grow;
The thundering avalanche crushes, loosened by only a breath,
And only a colourless drop may be laden with sudden death.

Only a word of command, but it loses or wins the field;
Only a stroke of the pen, but a heart is broken or healed;
Only a step may sever, pole-wide, future and past;
Only a touch may rivet links which for life shall last.

Only a look and a motion! Why was the wound so deep?
Were it no echo of sorrow, hushed for a while to sleep,
Were it no shadow of fear, far o'er the future thrown,
Slight were the suffering now, if it bore on the present alone.

Ah! I would smile it away, but 'tis all too fresh and too keen;
Perhaps I may some day recall it as if it had never been;
Now I can only be still, and endure where I cannot cope,
Praying for meekness and patience, praying for faith and hope.

Is it an answer already that words to my mind are brought,
Floating like shining lilies on waters of gloomiest thought?
Simple and short is the sentence, but oh! what it comprehends!
'*Those with which I was wounded, in the house of My friends.*'

Floating still on my heart, while I listen again and again,
Stilling the anxious throbbing, soothing the icy pain,
Proving its sacred mission healing and balm to bring.
'Coming?' Yes, if you want me! Yes, I am ready to sing.

Whose I Am.

JESUS, Master, whose I am,
    Purchased Thine alone to be,
By Thy blood, O spotless Lamb,
    Shed so willingly for me;

Let my heart be all Thine own,
Let me live to Thee alone.

Other lords have long held sway;
    Now, Thy name alone to bear,
Thy dear voice alone obey,
    Is my daily, hourly prayer.
Whom have I in heaven but Thee?
Nothing else my joy can be.

Jesus, Master! I am Thine;
    Keep me faithful, keep me near;
Let Thy presence in me shine
    All my homeward way to cheer.
Jesus! at Thy feet I fall,
Oh, be Thou my All-in-all.

Whom I Serve.

JESUS, Master, whom I serve,
    Though so feebly and so ill,
Strengthen hand and heart and nerve
    All Thy bidding to fulfil;
Open Thou mine eyes to see
All the work Thou hast for me.

Lord, Thou needest not, I know,
    Service such as I can bring;
Yet I long to prove and show
    Full allegiance to my King.
Thou an honour[1] art to me,
Let me be a praise to Thee.

Jesus, Master! wilt Thou use
    One who owes Thee more than all?
As Thou wilt! I would not choose,
    Only let me hear Thy call.
Jesus! let me always be
In Thy service glad and free.

[1] See marginal reading of 1 Peter 2:7.

Peace.

Is this the Peace of God, this strange, sweet calm?
The weary day is at its zenith still,
Yet 'tis as if beside some cool, clear rill,
    Through shadowy stillness rose an evening psalm,
And all the noise of life were hushed away,
And tranquil gladness reigned with gently soothing sway.

It was not so just now. I turned aside
With aching head, and heart most sorely bowed;
Around me cares and griefs in crushing crowd,
    While inly rose the sense, in swelling tide,
Of weakness, insufficiency, and sin,
And fear, and gloom, and doubt, in mighty flood rolled in.

That rushing flood I had no strength to meet,
Nor power to flee: my present, future, past,
My self, my sorrow, and my sin I cast
    In utter helplessness at Jesu's feet;
Then bent me to the storm, if such His will.
He saw the winds and waves, and whispered, 'Peace, be still!'

And there was calm! O Saviour, I have proved
That Thou to help and save art *really* near:
How else this quiet rest from grief, and fear,
    And all distress? The cross is not removed,
I must go forth to bear it as before,
But, leaning on Thine arm, I dread its weight no more.

Is it indeed Thy Peace? I have not tried
To analyze my faith, dissect my trust,
Or measure if belief be full and just,
    And therefore claim Thy Peace. But Thou hast died.
I know that this is true, and true for me,
And, knowing it, I come, and cast my all on Thee.

It is not that I feel less weak, but Thou
Wilt be my strength; it is not that I see
Less sin, but more of pardoning love with Thee,

And all-sufficient grace. Enough! And now
All fluttering thought is stilled, I only rest,
And feel that Thou art near, and know that I am blest.

God's Message.

To him that is far off.

PEACE, peace!
To him that is far away.
Turn, O wanderer! why wilt thou die,
When the peace is made that shall bring thee nigh?
Listen, O rebel! the heralds proclaim
The King's own peace through a Saviour's name;
Then yield thee to-day.

Peace, peace!
The word of the Lord to thee.
Peace, for thy passion and restless pride,
For thy endless cravings all unsupplied,
Peace for thy weary and sin-worn breast;
He knows the need who has promised rest,
And the gift is free.

Peace, peace!
Through Him who for all hath died!
Wider the terms than thy deepest guilt,
Or in vain were the blood of our Surety spilt:
Even *because* thou art far away
To thee is the message of peace to-day,
Peace through the Crucified.

AND TO HIM THAT IS NEAR.

PEACE, peace!
Yea, peace to him that is near.
The crown is set on the Victor's brow,
For thy warfare is accomplished now;
And for thee eternal peace is made
By the Lord on whom thy sins were laid:
Then why shouldst thou fear?

Peace, peace!
Wrought by the Spirit of Might.
In thy deepest sorrow and sorest strife,
In the changes and chances of mortal life,
It is thine, belovèd! Christ's own bequest,
Which vainly the Tempter shall strive to wrest;
It is now thy right.

Peace, peace!
Look for its bright increase;
Deepening, widening, year by year,
Like a sunlit river, strong, calm, and clear;
Lean on His love through this earthly vale,
For His word and His work shall never fail,
And 'He is our Peace.'

'A Great Mystery.'

THERE is a hush in earth and sky,
　　The ear is free to list aright
In darkness, veiling from the eye
　　The many-coloured spells of light.

Not heralded by fire and storm,
　　In shadowy outline dimly seen,
Comes through the gloom a glorious Form,
　　The once despisèd Nazarene.

Through waiting silence, voiceless shade,
　　A still, small Voice so clearly floats,
A listening lifetime were o'erpaid
　　By one sweet echo of such notes.

'Fear not, belovèd! thou art Mine,
　　For I have given My life for thee;
By name I call thee, rise and shine,
　　Be praise and glory unto Me.

'In Me all spotless and complete,
　　And in My comeliness most fair

Art thou; to Me thy voice is sweet,
　　Prevailing in thy feeblest prayer.

'Thy life is hid in God with Me,
　　I stoop to dwell within thy breast;
My joy for ever thou shalt be,
　　And in My love for thee I rest.

'O Prince's daughter, whom I see
　　In bridal garments, pure as light,
Betrothed for ever unto Me,
　　On thee My own new name I write.'

Lo! 'neath the stars' uncertain ray
　　In flowing mantle glistening fair,
One, lowly bending, turns away
　　From that sweet voice in cold despair.

Is it Humility, who sees
　　Herself unworthy of such grace,
Who dares not hope her Lord to please,
　　Who dares not look upon His face?

Nay, where that mantle fleeting gleams
　　'Tis Unbelief who turns aside,
Who rather rests in self-spun dreams,
　　Than trust the love of Him who died.

Faith casts away the fair disguise,
　　She will not doubt her Master's voice,
And droop when He hath bid her rise,
　　Or mourn when He hath said, 'Rejoice!'

Her stained and soilèd robes she leaves,
　　And Christ's own shining raiment takes;
What His love gives, her love receives,
　　And meek and trustful answer makes:

'Behold the handmaid of the Lord!
　　Thou callest, and I come to Thee:
According to Thy faithful word,
　　O Master, be it unto me!

'Thy love I cannot comprehend,
    I only know Thy word is true,
And that Thou lovest to the end
    Each whom to Thee the Father drew.

'Oh! take the heart I could not give
    Without Thy strength-bestowing call;
In Thee, and for Thee, let me live,
    For I am nothing, Thou art all.'

Be Not Weary.

Yes! He knows the way is dreary,
    Knows the weakness of our frame,
Knows that hand and heart are weary;
    He, 'in all points,' felt the same.
He is near to help and bless;
Be not weary, onward press.

Look to Him who once was willing
    All His glory to resign,
That, for thee the law fulfilling,
    All His merit might be thine.
Strive to follow day by day
Where His footsteps mark the way.

Look to Him, the Lord of Glory,
    Tasting death to win thy life;
Gazing on 'that wondrous story,'
    Canst thou falter in the strife?
Is it not new life to know
That the Lord hath loved thee so?

Look to Him who ever liveth,
    Interceding for His own:
Seek, yea, claim the grace He giveth
    Freely from His priestly throne.
Will He not thy strength renew
With His Spirit's quickening dew?

Look to Him, and faith shall brighten,
  Hope shall soar, and love shall burn;
Peace once more thy heart shall lighten
  Rise! He calleth thee, return!
Be not weary on thy way,
Jesus is thy strength and stay.

The Great Teacher.

I LOVE to feel that I am taught,
  And, as a little child,
To note the lessons I have learnt
  In passing through the wild.
For I am sure God teaches me,
  And His own gracious hand
Each varying page before me spreads,
  By love and wisdom planned.

I often think I cannot spell
  The lesson I must learn,
And then, in weariness and doubt,
  I pray the page may turn;
But time goes on, and soon I find
  I was learning all the while;
And words which seemed most dimly traced
  Shine out with rainbow smile.

Or sometimes strangely I forget,
  And, learning o'er and o'er,
A lesson all with tear-drops wet,
  Which I had learnt before.
He chides me not, but waits awhile,
  Then wipes my heavy eyes:
Oh what a Teacher is our God,
  So patient and so wise!

Dark silent hours of study fall,
  And I can scarcely see;
Then one beside me whispers low
  What is so hard to me.

'Tis easier then! I am so glad
　　I am not taught alone;
It is such help to overhear
　　A lesson like my own.

Sometimes the Master gives to me
　　A strange new alphabet;
I wonder what its use will be,
　　Or why it need be set.
And then I find this tongue alone
　　Some stranger ear can reach,
One whom He may commission me
　　For Him to train or teach.

If others sadly bring to me
　　A lesson hard and new,
I often find that helping them
　　Has made me learn it too.
Or, had I learnt it long before,
　　My toil is overpaid,
If so one tearful eye may see
　　One lesson plainer made.

We do not see our Teacher's face,
　　We do not hear His voice;
And yet we know that He is near,
　　We feel it, and rejoice.
There is a music round our hearts,
　　Set in no mortal key;
There is a Presence with our souls,
　　We know that it is He.

His loving teaching cannot fail;
　　And we shall know at last
Each task that seemed so hard and strange,
　　When learning time is past.
Oh! may we learn to love Him more,
　　By every opening page,
By every lesson He shall mark
　　With daily ripening age.

And then, to 'know as we are known'
    Shall be our glorious prize,
To see the Teacher who hath been
    So patient and so wise.
O joy untold! Yet not alone
    Shall ours the gladness be;
The travail of His soul in us
    Our Saviour-God shall see.

Auntie's Lessons.

THEY said their texts, and their hymns they sang,
    On that sunny Sabbath-day;
And yet there was time ere the church-bell rang,
    So I bid them trot away.
And leave me to rest and read alone,
Where the ash-tree's shade o'er the lawn was thrown.

But oh! 'twas a cry and a pleading sore,
    'O Auntie! we will not tease,
But tell us one Sunday story more;
We will sit so still on the grassy floor;
Tell us the one you told before
    Of little black Mumu, please,
Whom, deaf and dumb, and sick and lone,
    The good ship brought to Sierra Leone.'

Willie begged loud, and Francie low,
    And Alice, who could resist her?
Certainly not myself, and so
The story was just beginning, when lo!
    To the rescue came my sister.
'*I* will tell you a story to-day;
Aunt Fanny has all her own lessons to say!'

Wonderful notion, and not at all clear!
    Alfred looked quite astounded.
Who in the world *my* lessons could hear?

They guessed at every one far and near,
    'Twas a mystery unbounded.
They settled at last that it must be
Grandpapa Havergal over the sea.

Then merry eyes grew grave and wise,
    On tiptoe Alice trod;
She had a better thought than they,
And whispered low, 'Does Auntie say
    Her lessons all to God?'
How little the import deep she knew
Of those baby-words, so sweet and true!

Little she knew what they enfold!—
    A treasure of happy thought;
A tiny casket of virgin gold,
    With jewels of comfort fraught.
Great men's wisdom may pass away,
Dear Alice's words in my heart will stay.

Rest.

'Thou hast made us for Thyself, and the heart never resteth till it findeth rest
in Thee.'—*St. Augustine.*

MADE for Thyself, O God!
Made for Thy love, Thy service, Thy delight;
Made to show forth Thy wisdom, grace, and might;
Made for Thy praise, whom veiled archangels laud;
Oh strange and glorious thought, that we may be
    A joy to Thee!

Yet the heart turns away
From this grand destiny of bliss, and deems
'Twas made for its poor self, for passing dreams,
Chasing illusions melting day by day;
Till *for ourselves* we read on this world's best,
    'This is not rest!'

Nor can the vain toil cease,
Till in the shadowy maze of life we meet
One who can guide our aching, wayward feet
To find Himself, our Way, our Life, our Peace.
In Him the long unrest is soothed and stilled;
Our hearts are filled.

O rest, so true, so sweet!
(Would it were shared by all the weary world!)
'Neath shadowing banner of His love unfurled,
We bend to kiss the Master's piercèd feet;
Then lean our love upon His loving breast,
And know God's rest.

One Question, Many Answers.

'WHAT wouldst thou be?'
The question hath wakened wild thoughts in me,
And a thousand responses, like ghosts from their graves,
Arise from my soul's unexplored deep caves,
The echoes of every varying mood
Of a wayward spirit all unsubdued;
The voices which thrill through my inmost breast
May tell me of gladness, but not of rest.
What wouldst thou be?
'Tis well that the answer is not for me.

'What wouldst thou be?'
An eagle soaring rejoicingly.
One who may rise on the lightning's wing,
Till our wide, wide world seem a tiny thing;
Who may stand on the confines of boundless space,
And the giant form of the universe trace,
While its full grand harmonies swell around,
And grasp it all with mind profound.
Such would I be,
Only stayed by infinity.

'What wouldst thou be?'
A bright incarnation of melody.
One whose soul is a fairy lute,
Waking such tones as bid all be mute,
Breathing such notes as may silence woe,
Pouring such strains as make joy o'erflow,
Speaking in music the heart's deep emotion,
Soothing and sweet as the shell of the ocean.
        Such would I be,
Like a fountain of music, all pure and free.

        'What wouldst thou be?'
A living blossom of poesy.
A soul of mingled power and light,
Evoking images rare and bright,
Fair and pure as an angel's dream;
Touching all with a heavenly gleam;
And royally claiming from poet-throne
Earth's treasure of beauty as all mine own.
        Such would I be—
My childhood's dream in reality!

        'What wouldst thou be?'
A wondrous magnet to all I see.
A spirit whose power may touch and bind
With unconscious influence every mind;
Whose presence brings, like some fabled wand,
The love which a monarch may not command.
As the spring awakens from cold repose
The bloomless brier, the sweet wild rose.
        Such would I be,
With the love of all to encircle me.

        'What wouldst thou be?'
A wavelet just rising from life's wide sea.
I would I were once again a child,
Like a laughing floweret on mountains wild;
In the fairy realms of fancy dwelling,
The golden moments for sunbeams selling;

Ever counting on bright to-morrows,
And knowing nought of unspoken sorrows.
    Such would I be,
A sparkling cascade of untiring glee.

    'What wouldst thou be?'
A blessing to each one surrounding me;
A chalice of dew to the weary heart,
A sunbeam of joy bidding sorrow depart,
To the storm-tossed vessel a beacon light,
A nightingale song in the darkest night,
A beckoning hand to a far-off goal,
An angel of love to each friendless soul:
    Such would I be.
Oh that *such* happiness were for me!

    'What wouldst thou be?'
With these alone were no rest for me.
I would be my Saviour's loving child,
With a heart set free from its passions wild,
Rejoicing in Him and His own sweet ways;
An echo of heaven's unceasing praise,
A mirror here of His light and love,
And a polished gem in His crown above.
    Such would I be,
Thine, O Saviour, and one with Thee!

Content.

    '"What wouldst thou be?"
A wavelet just rising from life's wide sea.
I would I were once again a child,
Like a laughing floweret on mountains wild;
In the fairy realms of fancy dwelling,
The golden moments for sunbeams selling;
Ever counting on bright to-morrows,
And knowing nought of unspoken sorrows.
    Such would I be,
A sparkling cascade of untiring glee.'

    1860

.   .   .   .

Not so, not so!
For longings change as the full years flow.
When I had but taken a step or two
From the fairy regions still in view;
While their playful breezes fanned me still
At every pause on the steeper hill,
And the blossoms showered from every shoot,
Showered and fell, and yet no fruit,—
  It was grief and pain
That I never could be a child again.

  Not so, not so!
Back to my life-dawn I would not go.
A little is lost, but more is won,
As the sterner work of the day is done.
We forget that the troubles of childish days
Were once gigantic in morning haze.
There is less of fancy, but more of truth,
For we lose the mists with the dew of youth;
  And a rose is born
On many a spray which seemed only thorn.

  Not so, not so!
While the years of childhood glided slow,
There was all to receive and nothing to give:
Is it not better for others to live?
And happier far than merriest games
Is the joy of our new and nobler aims:
Then fair fresh flowers, *now* lasting gems;
Then wreaths for a day, but *now* diadems,
  For ever to shine,
Bright in the radiance of Love Divine.

  Not so, not so!
I would not again be a child, I know!
But were it not pleasant again to stand
On the border-line of that fairy land,—

Feeling so buoyant and blithe and strong,
Fearing no slip as we bound along,
Halting at will in the sunshine to bask,
Deeming the journey an easy task,
    While Courage and Hope
Smooth with 'Come, see, and conquer' each emerald slope?

    Not so, not so!
Less leaping flame, but a deeper glow!
There is more of sorrow, but more of joy,
Less glittering ore, but less alloy;
There is more of pain, but more of balm,
And less of pleasure, but more of calm;
Many a hope all spent and dead,
But higher and brighter hopes instead;
    Less risked, more won;
Less planned and dreamed, but perhaps more done.

    Not so, not so!
Not in stature and learning alone we grow.
Though we no more look from year to year
For power of mind more strong and clear,
Though the table-land of life we tread,
No widening view before we spread,
No sunlit summits to lure ambition,
But only the path of a daily mission,
    We would not turn
Where the will-o'-the-wisps of our young dreams burn.

    Then be it so!
For in better things we yet may grow.
Onward and upward still our way,
With the joy of progress from day to day;
Nearer and nearer every year
To the visions and hopes most true and dear;
Children still of a Father's love,
Children still of a home above!
    Thus we look back,
Without a sigh, o'er the lengthening track.

Misunderstood.

'People do not understand me,
　　Their ideas are not like mine;
All advances seem to land me
　　Still outside their guarded shrine.'

So you turn from simple joyance,
　　Losing many a mutual good,
Weary with the chill annoyance
　　So to be misunderstood.

Let me try to lift the curtain
　　Hiding other hearts from view;
You complain, but are you certain
　　That the fault is not with you?

In the sunny summer hours,
　　Sitting in your quiet room,
Can you wonder if the flowers
　　Breathe for you no sweet perfume?

True, you see them bright and pearly
　　With the jewelry of morn;
But their fragrance, fresh and early,
　　Is not through your window borne.

You must go to them, and stooping,
　　Cull the blossoms where they live;
On your bosom gently drooping,
　　All their treasure they will give.

Who would guess what fragrance lingers
　　In verbena's pale green show!
Press the leaflet in your fingers,
　　All its sweetness you will know.

Few the harps Æolian, sending
　　Unsought music on the wind:
Else must love and skill be blending
　　Music's full response to find.

'But my key-note,' are you thinking,
　'Will not modulate to theirs?'
Seek! and subtle chords enlinking,
　Soon shall blend the differing airs.

Fairly sought, some point of contact
　There must be with every mind;
And, perchance, the closest compact
　Where we least expect we find.

Perhaps the heart you meet so coldly
　Burns with deepest lava-glow;
Wisely pierce the crust, and boldly,
　And a fervid stream shall flow.

Dialects of love are many,
　Though the language be but one;
Study all you can, or any,
　While life's precious school-hours run.

Closed the heart-door of thy brother,
　All its treasure long concealed?
One key fails, then try another,
　Soon the rusty lock shall yield.

Few have not some hidden trial,
　And could sympathize with thine;
Do not take it as denial
　That you see no outward sign.

Silence is no certain token
　That no secret grief is there;
Sorrow which is never spoken
　Is the heaviest load to bear.

Seldom can the heart be lonely,
　If it seek a lonelier still,
Self-forgetting, seeking only
　Emptier cups of love to fill.

'Twill not be a fruitless labour,
  Overcome this ill with good;
Try to understand your neighbour,
  And you will be understood.

Sunbeams in the Wood.

MARK ye not the sunbeams glancing
  Through the cool green shade,
On the waving fern-leaves dancing,
  In the quiet glade?

See you how they change and quiver
  Where the broad oaks rise,
Rippling like a golden river
  From their fountain skies?

On the grey old timber resting
  Like a sleeping dove,
Like a fairy grandchild nesting
  In an old man's love.

On the dusty pathway tracing
  Arabesques with golden style;
Light and shadow interlacing,
  Like a tearful smile.

Many a hidden leaf revealing,
  Many an unseen flower;
Like a maiden lightly stealing
  Past each secret bower.

Oh! how beautiful they make it
  Everywhere they fall;
Sunbeams! why will ye forsake it
  At pale Evening's call?

In the arching thickets linger,
  In the woodland aisle,
Gilding them with trembling finger,
  Yet a little while.

Then, your last calm radiance pouring,
    Bid the earth good-night;
Like a sainted spirit soaring
    To a home of light.

The Star Shower.

NOVEMBER 14, 1866.

OH! to raise a mighty shout,
And bid the sleepers all come out!
No dreamer's fancy, fair and high,
Could image forth a grander sky.
And oh for eyes of swifter power
To follow fast the starry shower!
Oh for a sweep of vision clear
To grasp at once a hemisphere!

The solemn old chorale of Night,
With fullest chords of awful might,
Re-echoes still in stately march
Throughout the glowing heavenly arch:
But harmonies all new and rare
Are intermingling everywhere,
Fantastic, fitful, fresh, and free;
A sparkling wealth of melody,
A carol of sublimest glee,
Is bursting from the starry chorus,
In dazzling exultation o'er us.
O wondrous sight! so swift, so bright,
Like sudden thrills of strange delight;
As if the stars were all at play,
And kept ecstatic holiday;
As if it were a jubilee
Of glad millenniums fully told,
Or universal sympathy
With some new-dawning age of gold.

Flashing from the lordly Lion,
Flaming under bright Procyon,

From the farthest east up-ranging,
Past the blessed orb[1] unchanging;
Ursa's brilliance far out-gleaming,
From the very zenith streaming;
Rushing, as in joy delirious,
To the pure white ray of Sirius;
Past Orion's belted splendour,
Past Capella, clear and tender;
Lightening dusky Polar regions,
Brightening pale encircling legions;
Lines of fiery glitter tracing,
Parting, meeting, interlacing;
Paling every constellation
With their radiant revelation!
All we heard of meteor glory
Is a true and sober story;
Who will not for life remember
This night grandeur of November?

––––––––––

'Tis over now, the once-seen, dream-like sight!
With gradual hand the clear and breezy dawn
Hath o'er the marvels of the meteor night
A veil of light impenetrable drawn.
And earth is sweeping on through starless space,
Nor may we once look back, the shining field to trace.

Ere next the glittering stranger-throng we meet,
How many a star of life will seek the west!
Our century's dying pulse will faintly beat;
The toilers of to-day will be at rest;
And little ones, who now but laugh and play,
Will weary in the heat and burden of the day.

Oh, is there nothing beautiful and glad
But bears a message of decay and change?

[1] 'That admirable Polar Star, which is a *blessing* to astronomers.'—*Professor Airy's Popular Lectures on Astronomy.*

So be it! Though we call it stern and sad,
Viewed by the torch of Love, it is not strange.
'Tis mercy that in Nature's *every* strain
Deep warning tones peal out, in solemn sweet refrain.

And have not all created things a voice
For those who listen farther,—whispers low
To bid the children of the light rejoice
In burning hopes they yet but dimly know?
What will it be, all earthly darkness o'er,
To shine as stars of God for ever—evermore!

Treasure Trove.

I PLAYED with the whispering rushes,
    By a river of reverie,
Flowing so quietly onward
    Into an unknown sea.

And I watched the dreamy current,
    Till to my feet it brought,
Glistening among the pebbles,
    The pearl of a fair new thought.

New! yet many another,
    Leaning over the stream,
May have welcomed its sudden shining,
    And gazed on its gentle gleam.

Long it must have been lying,
    Yet it is new to me.
Oh the treasures around us,
    If we could only see!

I have broken the smooth dark water
    Into ripples and circles bright,
Lifting my pearl from the pebbles,
    Bearing away its light.

I am so glad to have found it!
　I shall treasure it safely a while,
It will brighten the niche that is darkest
　In my spirit's loneliest aisle.

And then, it may be, a dear one
　Will wear it, a long, long time,
Fastened firm on her bosom,
　In a setting of silver rhyme.

Coming Summer.

WHAT will the summer bring?
　Sunshine and flowers,
Brightness and melody,
　Golden-voiced hours;
Rose-gleaming mornings
　Vocal with praise;
Crimson-flushed evening,
　Nightingale lays.

What may the summer bring?
　Gladness and mirth,
Laughter and song,
　For the children of earth;
Smiles for the old man,
　Joy for the strong,
Glee for the little ones
　All the day long.

What will the summer bring?
　Coolness and shade,
Eloquent stillness
　In thicket and glade;
Whispering breezes,
　Fragrance oppressed;
Lingering twilight
　Soothing to rest.

What may the summer bring?
  Freshness and calm
To the care-worn and troubled,
  Beauty and balm.
O toil-weary spirit,
  Rest thee anew,
For the heat of the world-race
  Summer hath dew!

What will the summer bring?
  Sultry noon hours,
Lurid horizons,
  Frowning cloud-towers!
Loud-crashing thunders,
  Tempest and hail,
Death-bearing lightnings,
  It brings without fail.

What may the summer bring?
  Dimness and woe,
Blackness of sorrow
  Its bright days may know;
Flowers may be wormwood,
  Verdure a pall,
The shadow of death
  On the fairest may fall.

Is it not ever so?
  Where shall we find
Light that may cast
  No shadow behind?
Calm that no tempest
  May darkly await?
Joy that no sorrow
  May swiftly abate?

Will the story of summer
  Be written in light,
Or traced in the darkness
  Of storm-cloud and night?

We know not—we *would* not know
    Why should we quail?
Summer, we welcome thee!
    Summer, all hail!

September 1868.

An April burst of beauty,
    And a May like the Mays of old,
And a glow of summer gladness
    While June her long days told;
And a hush of golden silence
    All through the bright July,
Without one peal of thunder,
    Or a storm-wreath in the sky;
And a fiery reign of August,
    Till the moon was on the wane;
And then short clouded evenings,
    And a long and chilling rain.
I thought the summer was over,
    And the whole year's glory spent,
And that nothing but fog and drizzle
    Could be for Autumn meant;—
Nothing but dead leaves, falling
    Wet on the dark, damp mould,
Less and less of the sunshine,
    More and more of the cold.

But oh! the golden day-time;
    And oh! the silver nights;
And the scarlet touch on the fir trunks
    Of the calm, grand sunset lights;
And the morning's bright revealings,
    Lifting the pearly mist,
Like a bridal veil, from the valley
    That the sun hath claimed and kissed;
And oh! the noontide shadows
    Longer and longer now,

On the river margin resting,
    Like the tress on a thoughtful brow.
Rich fruitage bends the branches
    With amber, and rose, and gold,
O'er the purple and crimson asters,
    And geraniums gay and bold.

The day is warm and glowing,
    But the night is cool and sweet,
And we fear no smiting arrows
    Of fierce and fatal heat.
The leaves are only dropping,
    Like flakes of a sunset cloud,
And the robin's song is clearer
    Than Spring's own minstrel-crowd.
A soft new robe of greenness
    Decks every sunny mead,
And we own that bright September
    Is beautiful indeed.

Is thy life-summer passing?
    Think not thy joys are o'er!
Thou hast not seen what Autumn
    For thee may have in store.
Calmer than breezy April,
    Cooler than August blaze,
The fairest time of all may be
    September's golden days.
Press on, though summer waneth,
    And falter not, nor fear,
For God can make the Autumn
    The glory of the year.

Early Faith.

WHOM hear we tell of all the joy which loving Faith can bring,
The ever-widening glories reached on her strong seraph wing?
Is it not oftenest they who long have wrestled with temptation,
Or passed through fiery baptisms of mighty tribulation?

Perhaps, in life's great tapestry, the darkest scenes are where
The golden threads of Faith glance forth most radiant and fair;
And gazing on the coming years, which unknown griefs may bring,
We hail the lamp which o'er them all shall heavenly lustre fling.

Thank God! there is at eventide a gleam of ruby light,
A star of love amid the gloom of sorrow's lingering night,
An ivy-wreath upon the tomb, a haven in the blast,
A staff for weary, trembling ones, when youth and health are past.

But shall we seek the diamonds in the lone and dusky mine,
When 'mid the sunny sands of *youth* they wait to flash and shine?
Neglect the fountain of Christ's joy till woe-streams darkly flow,
Nor seek a Father's smile until the world's cold frown we know?

Nay! be our faith the rosy crown on morn's unwrinkled brow,
The sparkling dewdrop on the grass, the blossom on the bough;
The gleam of pearly light within the snowy-bosomed shell;
An added power of loveliness in beauty's every spell.

Oh, let it be the sunlight of the pleasant summer hours,
That calls to pure and radiant birth unnumbered fragrant flowers;
That bathes in golden joyance every anthem-murmuring tree,
And spreads a robe of glory o'er the silver-crested sea.

Oh, let it be the key-note of the symphony of gladness,
Which wots[1] not of the broken lyre, the requiem of sadness:
For they who melodies of heaven in hours of brightness know,
Will modulate sweet harmony from earth's discordant woe.

Our Father.

'OH that I loved the Father
    With depth of conscious love,
As stedfast, bright, and burning,
    As seraphim above!
But how can I be deeming
    Myself a loving child,
When here, and there, and everywhere,
    My thoughts are wandering wild?

[1] wots: knows

'It is my chief desire
   To know Him more and more,
To follow Him more fully
   Than I have done before:
My eyes are dim with longing
   To see the Lord above;
But oh! I fear from year to year,
   I do not truly love.

'For when I try to follow
   The mazes of my soul,
I find no settled fire of love
   Illumining the whole;
'Tis all uncertain twilight,
   No clear and vivid glow:
Would I could bring to God my King
   The perfect love I owe!'

The gift is great and holy,
   'Twill not be sought in vain;
But look up for a moment
   From present doubt and pain,
And calmly tell me *how* you love
   The dearest ones below?
'This love,' say you, 'is deep and true!'
   But tell me how you know?

How do you love your father?
   'Oh, in a thousand ways!
I think there's no one like him,
   So worthy of my praise.
I tell him all my troubles,
   And ask him what to do;
I know that he will give to me
   His counsel kind and true.

'Then every little service
   Of hand, or pen, or voice,
Becomes, if he has asked it,
   The service of my choice.

And from my own desires
    'Tis not so hard to part,
If once I know I follow so
    His wiser will and heart.

' I know the flush of pleasure
    That o'er my spirit came,
When far from home with strangers,
    They caught my father's name;
And for his sake the greeting
    Was mutual and sweet,
For if they knew my father too,
    How glad we were to meet!

' And when I heard them praising
    His music and his skill,
His words of holy teaching,
    Life-preaching, holier still,
How eagerly I listened
    To every word that fell!
'Twas joy to hear that name so dear
    Both known and loved so well.

' Once I was ill and suffering
    Upon a foreign shore,
And longed to see my father,
    As I never longed before.
He came: his arm around me;
    I leant upon his breast;
I did not long to feel more strong,
    So sweet that childlike rest.

' The thought of home is pleasant,
    Yet I should hardly care
To leave my present fair abode,
    Unless I knew him there.
All other love and pleasure
    Can never crown the place,
A home to me it cannot be
    Without my father's face.'

This is no fancy drawing,
   But every line is true,
And you have traced as strong a love
   As ever daughter knew.
But though its fond expression
   Is rather lived than told,
You do not say from day to day,
   'I fear my love is cold!'

You do not think about it;
   'Tis never in your thought—
'I wonder if I love him
   As deeply as I ought?
I know his approbation
   Outweighs all other meed,
That his employ is always joy
   But do I love indeed?'

Now let your own words teach you
   The higher, holier claim
Of Him, who condescends to bear
   A Father's gracious name.
No mystic inspiration,
   No throbbings forced and wild
He asks, but just the loving trust
   Of a glad and grateful child.

The rare and precious moments
   Of realizing thrill
Are but love's blissful blossom,
   To brighten, not to fill
The storehouse and the garner
   With ripe and pleasant fruit;
And not alone by these is shown
   The true and holy root.

What if your own dear father
   Were summoned to his rest!
One lives, by whom that bitterest grief
   Could well be soothed and blessed.

Like balm upon your sharpest woe
    His still small voice would fall;
His touch would heal, you could not feel
    That you had lost your all.

But what if He, the Lord of life,
    Could ever pass away!
What if *His* name were blotted out
    And you could know to-day
There was *no* heavenly Father,
    No Saviour dear and true,
No throne of grace, no resting-place,
    No living God for you!

We need not dwell in horror
    On what can never be,
Such endless desolation,
    Such undreamt misery.
Our reason could not bear it,
    And all the love of earth,
In fullest bliss, compared with this,
    Were nothing, *nothing* worth.

Then bring your poor affection,
    And try it by this test;
The hidden depth is fathomed,
    You see you love Him *best!*
'Tis but a feeble echo
    Of His great love to you,
Yet in His ear each note is dear,
    Its harmony is true.

It is an uncut jewel,
    All earth-encrusted now,
But He will make it glorious,
    And set it on His brow:
'Tis but a tiny glimmer,
    Lit from the light above,
But it shall blaze through endless days,
    A star of perfect love.

Disappointment.

Our yet unfinished story
   Is tending all to this:
To God the greatest glory,
   To us the greatest bliss.

If all things work together
   For ends so grand and blest,
What need to wonder whether
   Each in itself is best!

If some things were omitted
   Or altered as we would,
The whole might be unfitted
   To work for perfect good.

Our plans may be disjointed,
   But we may calmly rest;
What God has once appointed
   Is better than our best.

We cannot see before us,
   But our all-seeing Friend
Is always watching o'er us,
   And knows the very end.

What though we seem to stumble?
   He will not let us fall;
And learning to be humble
   Is not lost time at all.

What though we fondly reckoned
   A smoother way to go
Than where His hand has beckoned?
   It will be better so.

What only seemed a barrier
   A stepping-stone shall be;
Our God is no long tarrier,
   A present help is He.

And when amid our blindness
    His disappointments fall,
We trust His loving-kindness
    Whose wisdom sends them all.

They are the purple fringes
    That hide His glorious feet;
They are the fire-wrought hinges;
    Where truth and mercy meet.

By them the golden portal
    Of Providence shall ope,
And lift to praise immortal
    The songs of faith and hope.

From broken alabaster
    Was deathless fragrance shed,
The spikenard flowed the faster
    Upon the Saviour's head.

No shattered box of ointment
    We ever need regret,
For out of disappointment
    Flow sweetest odours yet.

The discord that involveth
    Some startling change of key,
The Master's hand resolveth
    In richest harmony.

We hush our children's laughter,
    When sunset hues grow pale;
Then, in the silence after,
    They hear the nightingale.

We mourned the lamp declining,
    That glimmered at our side;—
The glorious starlight shining
    Has proved a surer guide.

Then tremble not and shrink not
    When Disappointment nears;

Be trustful still, and think not
   To realize all fears.

While we are meekly kneeling,
   We shall behold her rise,
Our Father's love revealing
   An angel in disguise.

The Song Chalice.

'You bear the chalice.' Is it so, my friend?
   Have I indeed a chalice of sweet song,
   With underflow of harmony made strong
New calm of strength through throbbing veins to send?
I did not form or fill,—I do but spend
   That which the Master poured into my soul,
   His dewdrops caught in a poor earthen bowl,
That service so with praise might meekly blend.
May He who taught the morning stars to sing,
   Aye keep my chalice cool, and pure, and sweet,
And grant me so with loving hand to bring
   Refreshment to His weary ones,—to meet
Their thirst with water from God's music-spring;
   And, bearing thus, to pour it at His feet.

Silent in Love.

'He will rest[1] in his love.' ZEPHANIAH 3:17.

Love culminates in bliss when it doth reach
   A white, unflickering, fear-consuming glow;
   And, knowing it is known as it doth know,
Needs no assuring word or soothing speech.
It craves but silent nearness, so to rest,
   No sound, no movement, love not heard but felt,
   Longer and longer still, till time should melt,
A snow-flake on the eternal ocean's breast.

---

[1] Marginal reading—'*be silent.*'

Have moments of this silence starred thy past,
Made memory a glory-haunted place,
Taught all the joy that mortal ken can trace?
　　By greater light 'tis but a shadow cast;—
So shall the Lord thy God rejoice o'er thee,
And in His love will rest, and silent be.

Light and Shade.

LIGHT! emblem of all good and joy!
　　Shade! emblem of all ill!
And yet in this strange mingled life,
　　We need the shadow still.
A lamp with softly shaded light,
To soothe and spare the tender sight,
　　　　Will only throw
　　　　A brighter glow
Upon our books and work below.

We could not bear unchanging day,
　　However fair its light;
Ere long the wearied eye would hail,
As boon untold, the evening pale,
　　The solace of the night.
And who would prize our summer glow
If winter gloom we did not know?
　　　　Or rightly praise
　　　　The glad spring rays
Who never saw our rainy days?

How grateful in Arabian plain
　　Of white and sparkling sand,
The shadow of a mighty rock
　　Across the weary land!
And where the tropic glories rise,
Responsive to the fiery skies,
　　　　We could not dare
　　　　To meet the glare,
Or blindness were our bitter share.

Where is the soul so meek and pure,
   Who through his earthly days
Life's fullest sunshine could endure,
   In clear and cloudless blaze!
The sympathetic eye would dim,
And others pine unmarked by him,
     Were no chill shade
     Around him laid,
And light of joy could never fade.

He, who the light-commanding word
   Erst spake, and formed the eye,
Knows what that wondrous eye can bear,
And tempers with providing care,
By cloud and night, all hurtful glare,
   By shadows ever nigh.
So in all wise and loving ways
He blends the shadows of our days,
     To win our sight
     From scenes of night,
To seek the 'True and Only Light.'

We need some shadow o'er our bliss,
   Lest we forget the Giver:
So, often in our deepest joy
   There comes a solemn quiver;
We could not tell from whence it came,
   The subtle cause we cannot name;
     Its twilight fall
     May well recall
Calm thought of Him who gave us all.

There are who all undazzled tread
   Awhile the sunniest plain;
But they have sought the blessèd shade
By one great Rock of Ages made,
   A sure, safe rest to gain.
Unshaded light of earth soon blinds
To light of heaven sincerest minds:

O envy not
A cloudless lot!
We ask indeed we know not what.

So is it here, so is it now!
Not always will it be!
There is a land that needs no shade,
A morn will rise which cannot fade,
And we, like flame-robed angels made,
That glory soon may see.
No cloud upon its radiant joy,
No shadow o'er its bright employ,
No sleep, no night,
But perfect sight,
The Lord our Everlasting Light.

No Thorn Without a Rose.

'THERE is no rose without a thorn!'
Who has not found this true,
And known that griefs of gladness born
Our footsteps still pursue?

That in the grandest harmony
The strangest discords rise;
The brightest bow we only trace
Upon the darkest skies!

No thornless rose! So, more and more,
Our pleasant hopes are laid
Where waves this sable legend o'er
A still sepulchral shade.

But Faith and Love, with angel-might,
Break up life's dismal tomb,
Transmuting into golden light
The words of leaden gloom.

Reversing all this funeral pall,
White raiment they disclose;

Their happy song floats full and long,
　'No thorn without a rose!

'No shadow, but its sister light
　Not far away must burn!
No weary night, but morning bright
　Shall follow in its turn.

'No chilly snow, but safe below
　A million buds are sleeping;
No wintry days, but fair spring rays
　Are swiftly onward sweeping.

'With fiercest glare of summer air
　Comes fullest leafy shade;
And ruddy fruit bends every shoot,
　Because the blossoms fade.

'No note of sorrow but shall melt
　In sweetest chord unguessed;
No labour all too pressing felt,
　But ends in quiet rest.

'No sigh but from the harps above
　Soft echoing tones shall win;
No heart-wound but the Lord of Love
　Shall pour His comfort in.

'No withered hope, while loving best
　Thy Father's chosen way;
No anxious care, for He will bear
　Thy burdens every day.

'Thy claim to rest on Jesu's breast
　All weariness shall be,
And pain thy portal to His heart
　Of boundless sympathy.

'No conflict, but the King's own hand
　Shall end the glorious strife;
No death, but leads thee to the land
　Of everlasting life.'

Sweet seraph voices, Faith and Love!
    Sing on within our hearts
This strain of music from above,
    Till we have learnt our parts:

Until we see your alchemy
    On all that years disclose,
And, taught by you, still find it true,
    'No thorn without a rose!'

Yesterday, To-day, and For Ever.

A Greek Acrostic, thrice tripled.

Αει.[1]

A   h! the weary cares and fears,
E   arnest yearnings through the years!
I   s it not a vale of tears?

A   h! the love we gladly greet
E   ver now is incomplete;
I   f the melody be sweet,

A   nd the harmony be true,
E   arlier loss is more in view,
I   ll forebodings shadow through.

———

A   fter wintry frost and rime,
E   ven now, the heavenly chime
I   s a pledge of summer time.

A   nchorage within the veil,
E   ver stedfast, cannot fail,
I   f the wildest storms assail.

A   ngel songs of love are clearer,
E   arth is brighter, death is dearer,
I   f the heavenly home be nearer.

———

[1] For ever.

A ll in perfect union brought,
E very link which *God* has wrought
I n the chains of loving thought:

A ll our dear ones, far asunder,
E ach shall join the anthem-thunder
I n our future joy and wonder.

A ll shall come where nought shall sever,
E ndless meeting, parting never,
I n God's house to dwell for ever.

Christ's Recall.

RETURN!
O wanderer from My side!
Soon droops each blossom of the darkening wild,
Soon melts each meteor which thy steps beguiled,
Soon is the cistern dry which thou hast hewn,
And thou wilt weep in bitterness full soon.
Return! ere gathering night shall shroud the way
Thy footsteps yet may tread, in this accepted day.

Return!
O erring, yet beloved!
I wait to bind thy bleeding feet, for keen
And rankling are the thorns where thou hast been;
I wait to give thee pardon, love, and rest;
Is not My joy to see thee safe and blest?
Return! I wait to hear once more thy voice,
To welcome thee anew, and bid thy heart rejoice.

Return!
O fallen, yet not lost!
Canst thou forget the life for thee laid down,
The taunts, the scourging, and the thorny crown?
When o'er thee first My spotless robe I spread,
And poured the oil of joy upon thy head,
How did thy wakening heart within thee burn!
Canst thou remember all, and wilt thou not return?

Return!
O chosen of My love!
Fear not to meet thy beckoning Saviour's view;
Long ere I called thee by thy name, I knew
That very treacherously thou wouldst deal;
Now I have seen thy ways, yet I will heal.
Return! Wilt thou yet linger far from Me?
My wrath is turned away, I have redeemèd thee.

Faith's Question.

To whom, O Saviour, shall we go
        For life, and joy, and light?
No help, no comfort from below,
No lasting gladness we may know,
        No hope may bless our sight.
Our souls are weary and athirst,
But earth is iron-bound and cursed,
And nothing she may yield can stay
The restless yearnings day by day;
Yet, without *Thee*, Redeemer blest,
We *would* not, if we *could*, find rest.

To whom, O Saviour, shall we go?
        We gaze around in vain.
Though pleasure's fairy lute be strung,
And mirth's enchaining lay be sung,
        We dare not trust the strain.
The touch of sorrow or of sin
Hath saddened all, without, within;
What here we fondly love and prize,
However beauteous be its guise,
Has passed, is passing, or may pass,
Like frost-fringe on the autumn grass.

To whom, O Saviour, shall we go?
        Our spirits dimly wait
In the dungeon of our mortal frame;
And only one of direful name
        Can force its sin-barred gate.

Our loved ones can but greet us through
The prison gate, from which we view
All outward things. They enter not:
Thou, Thou alone, canst cheer our lot.
O Christ, we long for Thee to dwell
Within our solitary cell!

To whom, O Saviour, shall we go?
　　　Unless Thy voice we hear,
All tuneless falls the sweetest song,
And lonely seems the busiest throng
　　　Unless we feel Thee near.
We dare not think what earth would be,
Thou Heaven-Creator, but for Thee;
A howling chaos, wild and dark—
One flood of horror, while no ark,
Upborne above the gloom-piled wave,
From one great death-abyss might save.

To whom, O Saviour, shall we go?
　　　The Tempter's power is great;
E'en in our hearts is evil bound,
And, lurking stealthily around,
　　　Still for our souls doth wait.
Thou tempted One, whose suffering heart
In all our sorrows bore a part,
Whose life-blood only could atone,
Too weak are we to stand alone;
And nothing but Thy shield of light
Can guard us in the dreaded fight.

To whom, O Saviour, shall we go?
　　　The night of death draws near;
Its shadow must be passed alone,
No friend can with our souls go down
　　　The untried way to cheer.
Thou hast the words of endless life;
Thou givest victory in the strife;
Thou only art the changeless Friend,
On whom for aye we may depend:
In life, in death, alike we flee,
O Saviour of the world, to THEE.

'I Did This for Thee! What Hast Thou Done for Me?'

(MOTTO PLACED UNDER A PICTURE OF OUR SAVIOUR IN THE STUDY OF A GERMAN DIVINE.)

I GAVE My life for thee,	Galatians 2:20.
My precious blood I shed,	1 Peter 1:19.
That thou might'st ransomed be,	Ephesians 1:7.
And quickened from the dead.	Ephesians 2:1.
I gave My life for thee;	Titus 2:14.
What hast thou given for Me?	John 21:15–17.
I spent long years for thee	1 Timothy 1:15.
In weariness and woe,	Isaiah 53:3.
That an eternity	John 17:24.
Of joy thou mightest know.	John 16:22.
I spent long years for thee;	John 1:10, 11.
Hast thou spent *one* for Me?	1 Peter 4:2.
My Father's home of light,	John 17:5.
My rainbow-circled throne,	Revelation 4:3.
I left, for earthly night,	Philippians 2:7.
For wanderings sad and lone.	Matthew 8:20.
I left it all for thee;	2 Corinthians 8:9.
Hast thou left aught for Me?	Luke 10:29.
I suffered much for thee,	Isaiah 53:5.
More than thy tongue may tell,	Matthew 26:39.
Of bitterest agony,	Luke 22:44.
To rescue thee from hell.	Romans 5:9.
I suffered much for thee;	1 Peter 2:21–24.
What canst thou bear for Me?	Romans 8:17, 18.
And I have brought to thee,	John 4:10, 14.
Down from My home above,	John 3:13.
Salvation full and free,	Revelation 21:6.
My pardon and My love.	Acts 5:31.
Great gifts I brought to thee;	Psalm 68:18.
What hast thou brought to Me?	Romans 12:1.

Oh, let thy life be given,   Romans 6:13.
   Thy years for Him be spent,   2 Corinthians 5:15.
World-fetters all be riven,   Philippians 3:8.
   And joy with suffering blent;   1 Peter 4:13–16.
I gave Myself for thee: Ephesians 5:2.
Give thou *thyself* to Me!   Proverbs 23:26.

Isaiah 33:17.

THINE eyes shall see! Yes, thine, who, blind erewhile,
   Now trembling towards the new-found light dost flee,
Leave doubting, and look up with trustful smile—
     Thine eyes shall see!

Thine *eyes* shall see! Not in some dream Elysian,
   Not in thy fancy, glowing though it be,
Not e'en in faith, but in unveilèd vision,
     Thine *eyes* shall see!

Thine eyes *shall* see! Not on thyself depend
   God's promises, the faithful, firm, and free;
Ere they shall fail, earth, heaven itself, must end:
     Thine eyes *shall* see!

Thine eyes shall *see!* Not in a swift glance cast,
   Gleaning one ray to brighten memory,
But while a glad eternity shall last,
     Thine eyes shall *see!*

Thine eyes shall see *the* King! The very same
   Whose love shone forth upon the curseful tree,
Who bore thy guilt, who calleth thee by name;
     Thine eyes shall see!

Thine eyes shall see the *King!* the mighty One,
   The many-crowned, the Light-enrobed; and He
Shall bid thee share the kingdom He hath won,
     Thine eyes shall see!

And *in His beauty!* Stay thee, mortal song,
 The 'altogether lovely' One must be
Unspeakable in glory,—yet ere long
    Thine eyes shall see!

Yes! though the land be 'very far' away,
 A step, a moment, ends the toil for thee;
Then, changing grief for gladness, night for day,
    Thine eyes shall see!

God the Provider.

'My God shall supply all your need, according to His riches in glory by Christ Jesus.'—
Philippians 4:19.

Who shall tell our untold need,
 Deeply felt, though scarcely known!
Who the hungering soul can feed,
 Guard, and guide, but God alone?
Blessèd promise! while we see
Earthly friends must powerless be,
Earthly fountains quickly dry:
'*God*' shall all your need supply.

He hath said it! so we know
 Nothing less can we receive.
Oh that thankful love may glow
 While we restfully believe,—
Ask not *how,* but trust Him still;
Ask not *when,* but wait His will:
Simply on His word rely,
God '*shall*' all your need supply.

Through the whole of life's long way,
 Outward, inward need we trace;
Need arising day by day,
 Patience, wisdom, strength, and grace.
Needing Jesus most of all,
Full of need, on Him we call;
Then how gracious His reply,
God shall '*all*' your need supply!

Great our need, but greater far
    Is our Father's loving power;
He upholds each mighty star,
    He unfolds each tiny flower.
He who numbers every hair,
Earnest of His faithful care,
Gave His Son for us to die;
God shall all *'your'* need supply.

Yet we often vainly plead
    For a fancied good denied,
What we deemed a pressing need
    Still remaining unsupplied.
Yet from dangers all concealed,
Thus our wisest Friend doth shield;
No *good* thing will He deny,
God shall all your *'need'* supply.

Can we count redemption's treasure,
    Scan the glory of God's love?
Such shall be the boundless measure
    Of His blessings from above.
All we ask or think, and more,
He will give in bounteous store,—
He can fill and satisfy!
God shall all your need *'supply.'*[1]

One the channel, deep and broad,
    From the Fountain of the Throne,
Christ the Saviour, Son of God,
    Blessings flow through Him alone.
He, the Faithful and the True,
Brings us mercies ever new:
Till we reach His home on high,
'God shall all your need supply.'

[1] The Greek word is much stronger than the English,—πληρώσει—'will supply to the full,' 'fill up,' 'satisfy.'

Wait Patiently for Him.

God doth not bid thee wait
To disappoint at last;
A golden promise, fair and great,
In precept-mould is cast.
Soon shall the morning gild
The dark horizon-rim,
Thy heart's desire shall be fulfilled,
'*Wait* patiently for Him.'

The weary waiting times
Are but the muffled peals
Low precluding celestial chimes,
That hail His chariot-wheels.
Trust Him to tune thy voice
To blend with seraphim;
His 'Wait' shall issue in 'Rejoice!'
'Wait *patiently* for Him.'

He doth not bid thee wait,
Like drift-wood on the wave,
For fickle chance or fixèd fate
To ruin or to save.
Thine eyes shall surely see,
No distant hope or dim,
The Lord thy God arise for thee:
'Wait patiently *for Him.*'

This Same Jesus.

Acts 1:11.

'This same Jesus!' Oh! how sweetly
Fall those words upon the ear,
Like a swell of far off music,
In a nightwatch still and drear!

He who healed the hopeless leper,
   He who dried the widow's tear;
He who changed to health and gladness
   Helpless suffering, trembling fear;

He who wandered, poor and homeless,
   By the stormy Galilee;
He who on the night-robed mountain
   Bent in prayer the wearied knee;

He who spake as none had spoken,
   Angel-wisdom far above,
All-forgiving, ne'er upbraiding,
   Full of tenderness and love;

He who gently called the weary,
   'Come and I will give you rest!'
He who loved the little children,
   Took them in His arms and blest;

He, the lonely Man of sorrows,
   'Neath our sin-curse bending low;
By His faithless friends forsaken
   In the darkest hours of woe;—

'This *same* Jesus!' When the vision
   Of that last and awful day
Bursts upon the prostrate spirit,
   Like a midnight lightning ray;

When, else dimly apprehended,
   All its terrors seem revealed,
Trumpet knell and fiery heavens,
   And the books of doom unsealed;

Then, we lift our hearts adoring
   'This same Jesus,' loved and known,
Him, our own most gracious Saviour,
   Seated on the great white Throne;

He Himself, and 'not another,'
   He for whom our heart-love yearned

Through long years of twilight waiting,
  To His ransomed ones returned!

For this word, O Lord, we bless Thee,
  Bless our Master's changeless name;
Yesterday, to-day, for ever,
  Jesus Christ is still the Same.

Mary's Birthday.

SHE is at rest,
In God's own presence blest,
Whom, while with us, this day we loved to greet;
  Her birthdays o'er,
  She counts the years no more;
Time's footfall is not heard along the golden street.

When we would raise
A hymn of birthday praise,
The music of our hearts is faint and low;
  Fear, doubt, and sin
  Make dissonance within;
And pure soul-melody no child of earth may know.

That strange 'new song,'
Amid a white-robed throng,
Is gushing from her harp in living tone;
  Her seraph voice,
  Tuned only to rejoice,
Floats upward to the emerald-archèd throne.[1]

No passing cloud
Her loveliness may shroud,
The beauty of her youth may never fade;
  No line of care
  Her sealèd brow may wear,
The joy-gleam of her eye no dimness e'er may shade.

[1] Revelation 4:3.

No stain is there
Upon the robes they wear,
Within the gates of pearl which she hath passed;
Like woven light,
All beautiful and bright,
Eternity upon those robes no shade may cast.

No sin-born thought
May in that home be wrought,
To trouble the clear fountain of her heart;
No tear, no sigh,
No pain, no death, be nigh
Where she hath entered in, no more to 'know in part.'

Her faith is sight,
Her hope is full delight,
The shadowy veil of time is rent in twain:
Her untold bliss—
What thought can follow this!
To her to live was Christ, to die indeed is gain.

Her eyes have seen
The King, no veil between,
In blood-dipped vesture gloriously arrayed:
No earth-breathed haze
Can dim that rapturous gaze;
She sees Him face to face on whom her guilt was laid.

A little while,
And they whose loving smile
Had melted 'neath the touch of lonely woe,
Shall reach her home,
Beyond the star-built dome;
Her anthem they shall swell, her joy they too shall know.

Daily Strength.

'As thy days thy strength shall be!'
This should be enough for thee;
He who knows thy frame will spare
Burdens more than thou canst bear.

When thy days are veiled in night,
Christ shall give thee heavenly light;
Seem they wearisome and long,
Yet in Him thou shalt be strong.

Cold and wintry though they prove,
Thine the sunshine of His love,
Or, with fervid heat oppressed,
In His shadow thou shalt rest.

When thy days on earth are past,
Christ shall call thee home at last,
His redeeming love to praise,
Who hath strengthened all thy days.

The Right Way.

LORD, is it still the right way, though I cannot see Thy face,
Though I do not feel Thy presence and Thine all-sustaining grace?
Can even this be leading through the bleak and sunless wild
To the City of Thy holy rest, the mansions undefiled?

Lord, is it still the right way? A while ago I passed
Where every step seemed thornier and harder than the last;
Where bitterest disappointment and inly aching sorrow
Carved day by day a weary cross, renewed with every morrow.

The heaviest end of that strange cross I knew was laid on Thee;
So I could still press on, secure of Thy deep sympathy.
Our upward path may well be steep, else how were patience tried?
I knew it was the right way, for it led me to Thy side.

But now I wait alone amid dim shadows dank and chill;
All moves and changes round me, but I seem standing still;
Or every feeble footstep I urge towards the light
Seems but to lead me farther into the silent night.

I cannot hear Thy voice, Lord! dost Thou still hear my cry?
I cling to Thine assurance that Thou art ever nigh;
I know that Thou art faithful; I trust, but cannot see
That it is still the right way by which Thou leadest me.

I think I could go forward with brave and joyful heart,
Though every step should pierce me with unknown fiery smart,
If only I might see Thee, if I might gaze above
On all the cloudless glory of the sunshine of Thy love.

Is it really leading onwards? When the shadows flee away,
Shall I find this path has brought me more near to perfect day?
Or am I left to wander thus that I may stretch my hand
To some still wearier traveller in this same shadow-land.

Is this Thy chosen training for some future task unknown?
Is it that I may learn to rest upon Thy word alone?
Whate'er it be, oh! leave me not, fulfil Thou every hour
The purpose of Thy goodness, and the work of faith with power.

I lay my prayer before Thee, and, trusting in Thy word,
Though all is silence in my heart, I know that Thou hast heard.
To that blest City lead me, Lord (still choosing all my way),
Where faith melts into vision as the starlight into day.

Thy Will Be Done.

'Understanding *what* the will of the Lord is.'—EPHESIANS 5:17.

WITH quivering heart and trembling will
    The word hath passed thy lips,
Within the shadow, cold and still,
    Of some fair joy's eclipse.
'Thy will be done!' Thy God hath heard,
And He will crown that faith-framed word.

Thy prayer shall be fulfilled: but how?
    His thoughts are not as thine;
While thou wouldst only weep and bow,
    He saith, 'Arise and shine!'
Thy thoughts were all of grief and night,
But His of boundless joy and light.

Thy Father reigns supreme above:
 The glory of His name
Is Grace and Wisdom, Truth and Love,
 His will must be the same.
And thou hast asked all joys in one,
In whispering forth, 'Thy will be done.'

His will—each soul to sanctify
 Redeeming might hath won; [1]
His will—that thou shouldst never die,
 Believing on His Son; [2]
His will—that thou, through earthly strife,
Shouldst rise to everlasting life. [3]

That one unchanging song of praise
 Should from our hearts arise; [4]
That we should know His wondrous ways,
 Though hidden from the wise; [5]
That we, so sinful and so base,
Should know the glory of His grace. [6]

His will—to grant the yearning prayer
 For dear ones far away, [7]
That they His grace and love may share,
 And tread His pleasant way;
That in the Father and the Son
All perfect we may be in one. [8]

His will—the little flock to bring
 Into His royal fold,
To reign for ever with their King, [9]
 His beauty to behold. [10]
Sin's fell dominion crushed for aye,
Sorrow and sighing fled away.

---

[1] 1 Thessalonians 4:3. [5] Matthew 11:25, 26. [9] Luke 12:32.
[2] John 6:40. [6] Ephesians 1:5, 6, 11, 12. [10] Isaiah 33:17.
[3] John 6:39. [7] 1 John 5:14–16.
[4] 1 Thessalonians 5:18. [8] John 17:23, 24.

This thou hast asked! And shall the prayer
    Float upward on a sigh?
No song were sweet enough to bear
    Such glad desires on high!
But God thy Father shall fulfil,
In thee and for thee, all His will.

'The Things Which Are Behind.'

LEAVE behind earth's empty pleasure,
    Fleeting hope and changeful love;
Leave its soon-corroding treasure:
    There are better things above.

Leave, oh, leave thy fond aspirings,
    Bid thy restless heart be still;
Cease, oh, cease thy vain desirings,
    Only seek thy Father's will.

Leave behind thy faithless sorrow,
    And thine every anxious care;
He who only knows the morrow
    Can for thee its burden bear.

Leave behind the doubting spirit,
    And thy crushing load of sin;
By thy mighty Saviour's merit,
    Life eternal thou shalt win.

Leave the darkness gathering o'er thee,
    Leave the shadow-land behind;
Realms of glory lie before thee;
    Enter in, and welcome find.

'Now I See.'

JOHN 9:25.

'Now I see!' But not the parting
    Of the melting earth and sky,

Not a vision dread and startling,
    Forcing one despairing cry.
But I see the solemn saying,
    All have sinned, and all must die;
Holy precepts disobeying,
    Guilty all the world must lie.
Bending, silenced, to the dust,
Now I see that God is just.

'Now I see!' But not the glory,
    Not the face of Him I love,
Not the full and burning story
    Of the mysteries above.
But I see what God hath spoken,
    How His well-belovèd Son
Kept the laws which man hath broken,
    Died for sins which man hath done;
Dying, rising, throned above!
'Now I see' that God is Love.

Everlasting Love.

'Yea, I have loved thee with an everlasting love, *therefore* with loving-kindness have I drawn thee.'—JEREMIAH 31:3 'No man can come to Me except the Father which hath sent Me draw him.'—JOHN 6:44.

'GOD's everlasting love! What wouldst thou more?'
O true and tender friend, well hast thou spoken.
My heart was restless, weary, sad, and sore,
And longed and listened for some heaven-sent token:
And, like a child that knows not why it cried,
'Mid God's full promises it moaned, 'Unsatisfied!'

Yet there it stands. O love surpassing thought,
So bright, so grand, so clear, so true, so glorious;
Love infinite, love tender, love unsought,
Love changeless, love rejoicing, love victorious!
And this great love for us in boundless store:
God's everlasting love! What would we more?

Yes, one thing more! To know it ours indeed,
To add the conscious joy of full possession.
O tender grace that stoops to every need!
This everlasting love hath found expression
In loving-kindness, which hath gently drawn
The heart that else astray too willingly had gone.

From no less fountain such a stream could flow,
No other root could yield so fair a flower:
Had He not loved, He had not drawn us so;
Had He not drawn, we had nor will nor power
To rise, to come;—the Saviour had passed by
Where we in blindness sat without one care or cry.

We thirst for *God,* our treasure *is* above;
Earth has no gift our one desire to meet,
And that desire is pledge of His own love.
Sweet question; with no answer! oh *how* sweet!
My heart in chiming gladness o'er and o'er
Sings on—'God's everlasting love! What wouldst
    thou more?'

'Master, Say On!'

MASTER, speak! Thy servant heareth,
    Waiting for Thy gracious word,
Longing for Thy voice that cheereth;
    Master! let it now be heard.
I am listening, Lord, for Thee;
What hast Thou to say to me?

Master, speak in love and power:
    Crown the mercies of the day,
In this quiet evening hour
    Of the moonrise o'er the bay,
With the music of Thy voice;
Speak! and bid Thy child rejoice.

Often through my heart is pealing
    Many another voice than Thine,
Many an unwilled echo stealing
    From the walls of this Thy shrine:
Let Thy longed-for accents fall;
Master, speak! and silence all.

Master, speak! I do not doubt Thee,
    Though so tearfully I plead;
Saviour, Shepherd! oh, without Thee
    Life would be a blank indeed!
But I long for fuller light,
Deeper love, and clearer sight.

Resting on the 'faithful saying,'
    Trusting what Thy gospel saith,
On Thy written promise staying
    All my hope in life and death,
Yet I long for something more
From Thy love's exhaustless store.

Speak to me by name, O Master,
    Let me *know* it is to me;
Speak, that I may follow faster,
    With a step more firm and free,
Where the Shepherd leads the flock,
In the shadow of the Rock.

Master, speak! I kneel before Thee,
    Listening, longing, waiting still;
Oh, how long shall I implore Thee
    This petition to fulfil!
Hast Thou not one word for me?
Must my prayer unanswered be?

Master, speak! Though least and lowest,
    Let me not unheard depart;
Master, speak! for oh, Thou knowest
    All the yearning of my heart,
Knowest all its truest need;
Speak! and make me blest indeed.

Master, speak! and make me ready,
　　When Thy voice is truly heard,
With obedience glad and steady
　　Still to follow every word.
I am listening, Lord, for Thee;
Master, speak, oh, speak to me!

Remote Results.

WHERE are the countless crystals,
　　So perfect and so bright,
That robed in softest ermine
　　The winter day and night?
Not lost! for, life to many a root,
They rise again in flower and fruit.

Where are the mighty forests,
　　And giant ferns of old,
That in primeval silence
　　Strange leaf and frond unrolled?
Not lost! for now they shine and blaze,
The light and warmth of Christmas days.

Where are our early lessons,
　　The teachings of our youth,
The countless words forgotten
　　Of knowledge and of truth?
Not lost! for they are living still,
As power to think, and do, and will.

Where is the seed we scatter,
　　With weak and trembling hand,
Beside the gloomy waters,
　　Or on the arid land?
Not lost! for after many days
Our prayer and toil shall turn to praise.

Where are the days of sorrow,
　　And lonely hours of pain,

When work is interrupted,
    Or planned and willed in vain?
Not lost! it is the thorniest shoot
That bears the Master's pleasant fruit.

Where, where are all God's lessons,
    His teachings dark or bright?
Not lost! but only hidden,
    Till, in eternal light,
We see, while at His feet we fall,
The reasons and results of all.

On the Last Leaf.[1]

FINISHED at last!
    Yet for five years past
My book on the dusty shelf hath lain,
And I hardly thought that ever again
My thoughts would follow the pleasant chime
Of musical measure and ringing rhyme.

I remember well when I laid it by,
Closed with a sort of requiem sigh.
Spring in her beauty had swept along,
And left my spirit all full of song:
The wakening depths of my heart were stirred,
Voices within and without I heard,
    Whispering me
    That I might be
A messenger of peace and pleasure;
    That in my careless minstrelsy
Lay something of poetic treasure,
Which, wrought with care, I yet some day
At all my loved ones' feet might lay.
Perhaps 'twas a vain and foolish dream,
A fancy-lit, illusive gleam!

[1] Written at the close of a manuscript volume.

And yet I cannot quite believe
That such bright impulse could deceive.
I felt I had so much to say,
Such pleasant thoughts from day to day,
Sang, lark-like, with each morning ray,
Or murmured low in twilight grey,
    Like distant curfew pealing.
And then, for each, fair Fancy brought
A robe of language ready wrought,
The smile of every wingèd thought
    Half veiling, half revealing.
And I only waited, with longing gaze,
For the golden leisure of summer days,
Which I thought to crown with happiest lays.

God thought not so! Ah no, He knew
There was other work for me to do,
There were other lessons for me to learn:
Another voice fell, low and stern,
    Upon the too reluctant ear.
Before the solemn voice of Pain
My visions fled, nor came again,
With all their glad and lovely train,
    My summer-tide to cheer.

Well is it when, at high command
Of wisest Love, she takes her stand
    At the heart's busy portal,
And warns away each noisy guest
Whose presence chases calm and rest,
Our powers, the brightest and the best,
    Proclaiming weak and mortal.
That so the way may be more clear
    For Him, the Prince of Peace, to come,
That which is left all void and drear
    To make His palace and His home.

And so the song of my heart was hushed,
    And the chiming thoughts were stilled:

Summer flew by, but the hope was crushed,
Swiftly onward my life-tide rushed,
    But my book remained unfilled.
For an aching head and a weary frame,
Poetry is but an empty name.
Yet I am sure it was better so,
I *trusted* then, and now I *know*.

For ever, I think, the gift is fled
    Which once I fancied mine:
So be it! A 'name' is not for me;
Loving and loved I would rather be,
With power to cheer and sympathize,
Bearing new light for tear-dimmed eyes;
    But I do not care to shine.

So if aught I write may tend to this,
My fairest hope of earthly bliss,
    Content with humblest rhyme I'll be;
And, striving less and trusting more,
All simple, earnest thoughts outpour,
    Such as my God may give to me.

How Should They Know Me?

THERE are those who deem they know me well,
    And smile as I tell them 'nay!'
Who think they may clearly and carelessly tell
Each living drop in my heart's deep well,
And lightly enter its inmost cell;
    But little (how little!) know they!

How should they know me? My soul is a maze
    Where I wander alone, alone;
Never a footfall there was heard,
Never a mortal hand hath stirred
The silence-curtain that hangs between
Outer and inner, nor eye hath seen
    What is only and ever my own.

They have entered indeed the vestibule,
    For its gate is opened wide,
High as the roof, and I welcome all
Who will visit my warm reception-hall,
And utter a long and loving call
    To some who are yet outside.

I would lead each guest to a place of rest;
    All should be calm and bright;
Then a lulling flow of melody,
And a crystal draught of sympathy,
And odorous blossoms of kindly thought,
With golden fruit of deed, be brought
    From the chambers out of sight.

Some I would take with a cordial hand,
    And lead them round the walls;
Showing them many a storied screen,
Many a portrait, many a scene,
Deep-cut carving, and outlined scroll;
Passing quickly where shadows roll,
    Slowly where sunshine falls.

They do not know and they cannot see
    That strong-hinged, low-arched door,
Though I am passing in and out,
From gloom within to light without,
Or from gloom without to light within;
None can ever an entrance win,
    None! for evermore.

It is a weird and wondrous realm,
    Where I often hold my breath
At the unseen things which there I see,
At the mighty shapes which beckon to me,
At the visions of woe and ecstasy,
    At the greetings of life and death.

They rise, they pass, they melt away,
    In an ever-changing train;

I cannot hold them or tell their stay,
Or measure the time of their fleeting sway;
As grim as night, and as fair as day,
    They vanish and come again.

I wander on through the strange domain,
    Marvelling ever and aye;
Marvelling how around my feet
All the opposites seem to meet,
The dark, the light, the chill, the glow,
The storm, the calm, the fire, the snow,—
How can it be? I do not know.
    Then how, oh how, can they?

What am I, and how? If reply there be,
    In unsearchable chaos 'tis cast.
Though the soaring spirit of restless man
Might the boundary line of the universe scan,
And measure and map its measureless plan,
    The gift of self-knowledge were last!

Making Poetry.

LITTLE one, what are you doing,
    Sitting on the window-seat?
Laughing to yourself, and writing,
Some right merry thought inditing,
    Balancing with swinging feet.

' 'Tis some poetry I'm making,
    Though I never tried before:
Four whole lines! I'll read them to you.
Do you think them funny, do you?
    Shall I try to make some more?

' I should like to be a poet,
    Writing verses every day;
Then to you I'd always bring them,
You should make a tune and sing them;
    'T would be pleasanter than play.'

Think you, darling, nought is needed
    But the paper and the ink,
And a pen to trace so lightly,
While the eye is beaming brightly,
    All the pretty things we think?

There's a secret,—can you trust me?
    Do not ask me what it is!
Perhaps some day you too will know it,
If you live to be a poet,
    All its agony and bliss.

Poetry is not a trifle,
    Lightly thought and lightly made;
Not a fair and scentless flower,
Gaily cultured for an hour,
    Then as gaily left to fade.

'Tis not stringing rhymes together
    In a pleasant true accord;
Not the music of the metre,
Not the happy fancies, sweeter
    Than a flower-bell, honey-stored.

'Tis the essence of existence,
    Rarely rising to the light;
And the songs that echo longest,
Deepest, fullest, truest, strongest,
    With your life-blood you will write.

With your life-blood. None will know it,
    You will never tell them how.
Smile! and they will never guess it:
Laugh! and you will not confess it
    By your paler cheek and brow.

There must be the tightest tension
    Ere the tone be full and true;
Shallow lakelets of emotion
Are not like the spirit-ocean,
    Which reflects the purest blue.

Every lesson you shall utter,
    If the charge indeed be yours,
First is gained by earnest learning,
Carved in letters deep and burning
    On a heart that long endures.

Day by day that wondrous tablet
    Your life-poem shall receive,
By the hand of Joy or Sorrow;
But the pen can never borrow
    Half the records that they leave.

You will only give a transcript
    Of a life-line here and there,
Only just a spray-wreath springing
From the hidden depths, and flinging
    Broken rainbows on the air.

Still, if you but copy truly,
    'T will be poetry indeed,
Echoing many a heart's vibration,
Rather love than admiration
    Earning as your priceless meed.

Will you seek it? Will you brave it?
    'Tis a strange and solemn thing,
Learning long, before your teaching,
Listening long, before your preaching,
    Suffering before you sing.

The Cascade.

WHO saith that Poetry is not in thee,
Thou wild cascade, bright, beautiful, and free?
Who saith that thine own sunny gleaming waters
Are not among 'sweet Poesie's' fair daughters?
No Poetry in thee? then tell, oh tell,
Where is the home where she delights to dwell?
But what is Poetry? Some aerial sprite,

Clothed in a dazzling robe of wavy light,
Whose magic touch unlocks the gates of joy
In dreamland to some vision-haunted boy?
Or is she but a breath from Eden-bowers,
Charged with the fragrance of their shining flowers,
Which, passing o'er the harp-strings of the soul,
Awakes new melody, whose echoes roll
In waves of spirit-music through the heart,
Till tears and smiles in mingling sweetness start?
It may be so, but still she seems to me
Most like a God-sent sunlight, rich and free,
Bathing the tiniest leaf in molten gold,
Bidding each flower some secret charm unfold,
Weaving a veil of loveliness for earth,
Calling all fairy forms to wondrous birth.

Our sweet soul-Artist! Many a fair surprise
Her colour-treasures bring to waiting eyes;
Her pictures, sudden seen, oft seem to dwell
Like pearls within the rugged ocean shell,
They tell of something purer and more fair
Than earth can boast, and gleam forth everywhere,
Star-glimpses through the trees, or flashes bright
Of meteor glory in a northern night.

Our sweet soul-Harpist! linking winds with sighs,
And blending both with spirit-melodies,
And adding chords that come we know not whence,
Dream-echoes mingling with the wakeful sense.
O strange, O beautiful! though all unknown,
The music-fount of every lovely tone,
The colour-fount of every lovely thought,
By this bright ministrant so freely brought,
Save that we own their true and soothing might
One of His perfect gifts, whose names are Love and Light.

Oh! she is often where we least surmise,
And scorns the dimness of our heavy eyes;
We catch the ruby sparkles of her wing,
And she is gone like dewdrops of the spring;

Again, to glad us with her smile she stays,
And shows her brightness to our loving gaze.
No cave so dark but she may gain its porch,
And gild the shadows with her quenchless torch;
No dell so silent but her pealing voice
Can bid a leafy orchestra rejoice;
No waste so lonely but she there may hold
Her gorgeous court in splendour all untold.
And where those waters murmur as they leap,
A song of gentleness, and calm, and sleep,
Within the sounding music of their tone
I hear a voice, and know it is her own.

And where the fair, fond sunbeams blithely play
Amid the hazy wreaths of dancing spray,
A form of fairy grace shines forth to me;
I hail the vision, for I know 'tis she.
She loves that changeful, yet unchanging foam,
Within its arching bowers she finds a home,
And reads beneath its roof of fleeting snow
The secrets of the shadowy depth below.
Then who shall say that she is not in thee,
Thou wild cascade, bright, beautiful, and free!

Constance De V—.

AN EPISODE IN THE LIFE OF CHARLES MAURICE, PRINCE DE TALLEYRAND.

YE maidens of Old England!
    The joyous and the free,
The loving and the loved of all,
    Wherever ye may be;
Who wander through the ferny dell,
    And o'er the breezy hill,
And glide along the woodland path
    All at your own sweet will;
Who know the many joys of home,
    The song, the smile, the mirth,
The happy things which God has given
    To brighten this our earth:

Comes there a sigh, a longing thought,
  In lonely musing hours?
Deem ye there is a fairer realm,
  A purer faith than ours?
O cast away the yearning dream,
  And listen, while I tell
Of one who knew no other home
  Than her own convent cell.

I.

The rain comes down relentlessly,
  The sky is robed in grey,
Oh, Paris is a dreary place
  On such a dreary day!
But dreariest of the darkening streets,
  Where the loud rain doth fall,
Is that where looms the convent tower,
  Where frowns the convent wall.

II.

A boyish step is passing
  Beneath the dripping eaves,
With monkish lore beladen,
  With musty Latin leaves.
Ah, Charles Maurice, the young abbé,
  Thou art of princely birth!
For thee shall dawn a brighter day,
A strange high part be thine to play,
With wondrous tact to guide and sway
  The great ones of the earth!

III.

But the still-increasing torrents
  Will spoil the ancient tomes,
And woe betide Charles Maurice
  From the wrath of cowlèd gnomes!

So he seeks a low-bent archway
    Within the grim old wall,
Where never the laughing footstep
    Of a sunbeam dares to fall.

IV.

Anon he wraps the volumes
    In the folds of his hooded gown ;
Then starts to hear, though he knows no fear,
A sound which tells him life is near—
    That he is not alone.
He turns—the passage is dark as night,
    He listens—but all is still,
Save the raindrops in monotonous march,
And the ceaseless drip from the mouldering arch,
    On the stone so damp and chill.

V.

'*Qui vive?*' he cries right gaily,
    Through the cavernous entry's gloom ;
But a low, faint cry is the sole reply,
As the voice of one who is come to lie
    On the brink of a yawning tomb.
Oh, where is the true-hearted lad,
    Who at the call of sorrow
But in his thoughtlessness is glad
To help the weak and cheer the sad,
    And promise a brighter morrow ?

VI.

The cry was one of weakness—
    Of weariness unblest ;
And a pulse of gentle sympathy
    Makes music in his breast.
Through the dark way he gropeth
    To the iron-studded door,
Behind whose oaken grimness
Some dwell in cloistral dimness
    Who may pass out no more.

VII.

There, in the glimmering darkness,
    He deems he can descry
A small and sable-robèd form
    On the cold doorstep lie.
The form is that of maidenhood;
    And, in that boyish heart,
It wakes a helpful tenderness,
Like that which, hidden, yet doth bless
Through a loved brother's fond caress,
    Ere childhood's hours depart.

VIII.

'What is it?' said Charles Maurice,
    In a softly pitying tone;
'What dost thou fear? why art thou here?
    And why that weary moan?'
Then, lifting her with gentle arm,
    He bore her where the light
Fell on a girlish face so fair,
It seemed a seraph light to wear,
But for the sorrow mantling there,
    And the glance of wild affright.

IX.

Why should I paint her beauty?
    Have ye not often tried
To tell of rosy lip and cheek,
Of starlit eyes that shine and speak,
Of cloudlike locks that vainly seek
    The snowy brow to hide?
And feel ye not, when all is said
    That words can ever say,
The fount of beauty still is sealed—
The loveliness is not revealed
    To those who list the lay.

X.

Oh, words can never satisfy—
     They are too hard and real;
The subtle charm they cannot show
By which the Beautiful we know,
     The Beautiful we feel.
Perchance they speak the form, the mind,
     And draw the likeness well;
But at the closèd entrance gate
All reverently they bend and wait
     Where, 'neath the marble-arching dome,
In crystal-windowed palace-home,
     The soul itself doth dwell.

XI.

And who may tell how lovely
     The gentle Constance seemed,
When through such clouds of sorrow
     Her meteor beauty gleamed!
What wonder that all speechless,
     As in a trance of gladness,
The young abbé stood wonderingly,
     Before such radiant sadness?

XII.

For the look of hopeless terror
     Was softened as she raised
Those orbs of strange, quick brightness,
     And on Charles Maurice gazed.
She saw the pledge of kindness
     Traced on that high fair brow;—
'Oh, no! thou never wilt betray,
But aid thou canst not; say, oh say,
Am I not lost? There is no way
     Of safe return, I know.'

XIII.

Then the trembling hands she folded
    Over the burning cheek,
A wild and woe-born sobbing
    Forbade the lips to speak;
Till quiet words of sympathy,
    So softly breathed and low,
And the touch of that young hand on hers,
    Soon bade her story flow.

XIV.

'I was a very little child,
    Not old enough to know,
Perhaps kind looks had on me smiled,
    But I forget them now,
When I was brought to live so coldly here,
Where all goes on the same through weary month
    and year.

XV.

'I did not know how lovely all
    The world without must be;
The sunbeams on the convent wall
    Were quite enough for me;
But others came who knew, and then they told
Of all that I had dreamt, but never might behold.

XVI.

'They told me of the mountains tall,
    Where they might freely roam;
They told me of the waterfall,
    With music in its foam;
They told me of wide fields and opening flowers,
Of sloping mossy banks and glowing autumn bowers.

XVII.

'Of other things they told me, too,
        More beautiful to them,
Of gleaming halls where sparklets flew
        From many a radiant gem;
And then they told of mirth, and dance, and song.
Would I had never heard, that I might never long!

XVIII.

'They said the sky was just as blue
        Above the convent towers,
As where the arching forests threw
        A shade o'er summer flowers;
But I grew weary of that dazzling sky,
And longed to wander forth, e'en if it were to die.

XIX.

'I did not want to change my lot,
        I knew it might not be;
I only longed to have one spot
        All bright with memory.
To gaze just once upon the world I tried,
And then I would return to be Heaven's lonely bride.

XX.

'But, oh, I heard no sounds of mirth,
        No beauty I could see;
I could not find the lovely earth,
        It was not made for me.
And now my punishment indeed is sore,
My only home hath closed on me its iron door.'

XXI.

Yes! in her fevered restlessness
        She left her unwatched cell,
When all around were summoned
        By the deep-voiced matin-bell.

And in the damp-stoned cloisters
　　To rest awhile she thought,
Where cold, fresh air might round her play,
The burning fever pass away,
And coolness of the early day
　　To her hot brow be brought.

XXII.

Strange carelessness! no massy bar
　　Across the gate was thrown!
She deemed that world of beauty near;
She gazed around in haste and fear,
Oh, none were there to see and hear—
　　The timid bird has flown!
But the rain came down relentlessly,
　　The sky was robed in grey;
All dreary seemed the narrow street,
And nothing bright or fair might meet
Her of the white and trembling feet;
No loveliness is there to greet
　　That wandering star to-day.

XXIII.

Then, bowed with shame and weakness,
　　And disappointed hope
She only reached the heavy door
To find it firmly closed once more;
Ah, who shall help, and who restore,
　　And who that door shall ope?
The strong young arm of Charles Maurice
　　Tries once and yet again,
But the weighty portal baffles him:
　　Ah! is it all in vain?

XXIV.

But Constance darts one upward glance
　　Of blent despair and trust;

There is no bolt, for daylight gleams
Between the scarcely-meeting beams:
Some unknown obstacle there seems,
    And conquer it he must.
He strains his utmost strength, the sweat
    Is beading on his brow;
It creaks—it yields! O Constance, smile,
    The door is open now!

XXV.

From her cheek the flush hath faded,
    As fades the evening glow,
In pristine whiteness leaving
    The rosy Alpine snow.
And like a breeze of twilight
    The aspen-leaves among,
A whisper falls upon his ear
    From quivering lip and tongue:

XXVI.

'Farewell! Oh, thou hast saved me!'
    And the hand so white and cold,
With lingering clasp of gratitude,
    Her wordless thanks hath told.
One moment on that small, fair hand
    His youthful lips are pressed;
There is a reverence in his eye,
For grief and beauty both are nigh;
She passes like a spirit by,
    To seek her cheerless rest.

XXVII.

They are parted, like the dewdrops
    That linger in the smile
Of a storm-begotten rainbow,
    But for a little while:
Then one in lonely dimness
    To earth may soon descend;

And one with the bright sky above,
    Though all unseen, may blend.

XXVIII.

The young abbé hath paused in vain
    To hear her footstep pass;
'Twas lighter than the noiseless fall
    Of rose-leaf on the grass.
No sound is heard but the pattering rain,
    And he slowly turns away,
With the brown old books beneath his gown,
To meet his abbot's gathering frown,
    For loitering on the way.

XXIX.

Think you he conned the loveless lore
    Without a thoughtful sigh
For the loveliness in sorrow,
    Which passed so trance-like by?
Among the missal borders
    Was no such angel-face;
And such, once seen, fade not away;
Their image shines without decay,
When on the canvas of the heart,
With untaught skill, yet mystic art,
    Each line of light we trace.

XXX.

The wing of Time seems broken now,
    So tardy is his flight;
He deems by day that she is dead,
    He dreams she lives, by night.
Till quick anxiety hath found
    A messenger to bear
The tidings that he strove to frame,
    From woven hope and fear.

XXXI.

What wonder that he heard not
　　Her footfall on the stone!
She sank beneath the cloister wall,
　　Unheeded and alone;
And ere Charles Maurice stood again
　　Beneath the open sky,
For ever on the things of earth
　　She closed her weary eye.

XXXII.

Constance, the beautiful, hath left
　　Her dismal convent cell;
She hath not known one hope fulfilled,
One granted joy, one longing stilled.
For her the melody of life
Was but one chord of inward strife,
　　Was but one ruthless knell.
Her heart bedimmed with sameness,
　　Her only wish denied,
Oh, what a mockery it were
Her lot should such a title bear,
　　'Heaven's own appointed bride!'

XXXIII.

Why should her early spring-time
　　Be quenched in wintry gloom?
Was it not merciful and wise
To call her spirit to the skies
　　From such a living tomb?
How might that gentle maiden
　　Have scattered joy around,
And made the earth a brighter place,
For all her radiance and grace!
But now, unsorrowed and unknown,
Her only memory is a stone
　　Within the convent bound.

Fairy Homes.

I'VE found at last the hiding-place
    Where the fairy people dwell,
And to win the secrets of their race
    I hold the long-sought spell.

With the woodland fairies I can talk,
    I can list their silvery lays;
Oh! pleasant in a lonely walk
    Is the company of fays.

No fabled fancy 'tis to me,
    For in every floweret's bell
Is a tiny chamber, where I see
    A gentle fairy dwell.

And at my bidding forth they come,
    To soothe me or to cheer,
And to tell me tales of fairydom
    With voices soft and clear.

Full many a beauteous lesson, too,
    Their rosy lips can teach;
Great men would wonder if they knew
    How well the fairies preach!

When thoughts of sorrow sadden me,
    They seem to sympathize,
And gaze upon me lovingly,
    With tender earnest eyes;

But when a tide of joyous glee
    Is bringing song and smile,
Then brightly they look up to me,
    And laugh with me awhile.

Oh! lovely are the floweret homes
    Of these sweet summer fays;
God's thoughts of beauty taking form
    To gladden mortal gaze.

More Music.

Oh for a burst of song,
Exultant, deep, and strong,
One gush of music's billowy might,
To bear my soul away
Into the realms of day,
From these dim glacier-caves of Life's cold night!

Oh for a sunset strain
Wafted o'er slumberous main,
To enter, spirit-like, my prisoned heart,
And there, with viewless hand,
Unloose each mortal band,
That in the songs of heaven I too might learn a part.

The sweetest music here
Calls forth the quiet tear,
For grief and gladness flow in blended stream;
Oh for the joyous day,
(Can it be far away?)
When one great Alleluia song shall chase Life's tuneless dream!

Travelling Thoughts.

ON BOARD THE STEAMER LA FRANCE, JANUARY 26, 1866.

A STILL grey haze around us,
Behind, a foreign shore,
A still grey deep beneath us,
And Dover cliffs before.
Not one within a hundred miles
Whose name I ever heard,
None who would care to speak to me
A passing friendly word:
Yet not a shadow crosseth me
Of loneliness or fear;
I bless the Omnipresent One,
I know that God is here.

All whom I love are scattered:
    And many a month and mile
Rise, mountain-like, before, behind,
    Between me and their smile.
Oh that the love I bear them
    Might blossom into skill
To comfort and to brighten,
    And all with gladness fill!
Ah! helpless love! Yet 'tis a joy
    To turn each wish to prayer,
And, where each loved one sojourneth,
    To know that God is there.

The nearest and the dearest
    Are where the rushing Rhine
Bends northward from the Drachenfels,
    From castle, rock, and vine;
Where long-lined chestnut shadows
    Make tracery below,
And the moss-framed window challenges
    The might of frost and snow.
Lit rather by the dawn of heaven
    Than earthly sunset glow,
That passing home of faith and prayer!
    Oh, God is there, I know!

From thence the wing of loving thought
    Speeds on where Severn flows,
And hovers o'er as fair a scene
    As our fair England knows;
The home of summer roses,
    Of winter mirth and glee,—
Long may that home unbroken,
    That mirth unsilenced be!
The blessings of unbounded grace
    I pray Him to bestow,
And trust Him for the coming years,
    For He is there, I know.

Now westward sweeps the vision
    Across the Irish Sea,
And echoes low of sisters' love
    Come back again to me.
A beacon bright in stormy night
    Of error, rage, and wrong,
That home of love and truth shall cast
    Its radiance pure and strong.
They tell of rumours strange and dark;
    But oh! no need to fear!
God will not leave His own, I know,
    His guardian hand is near.

Another scene by gentle Ouse
    Must aye be dear to me,
Though all are not together now,
    And one is on the sea.
And where a grey cathedral tower
    Uprises broad and high,
A home is made in cloistral shade,
    Beside the winding Wye.
To seek the richest boons for these,
    Why should the heart be slow?
One Shepherd, Chief, and Great, and Good,
    Is watching there, I know.

Then, in a busy city,
    A crypt all dark and lone,
A name engraven on our hearts
    Is traced upon a stone.
Not *there* the sainted spirit!
    She dwells in holy light,
Within the pearl-raised portals,
    With those who walk in white.
May all her children follow
    The path she meekly trod,
And reach the home she rests in now,
    And dwell, like her, with God.

New Year's Wishes.

A PEARL-STREWN pathway of untold gladness,
Flecked by no gloom, by no weary sadness,
    Such be the year to thee!
A crystal rivulet, sunlight flinging,
Awakening blossoms, and joyously singing
    Its own calm melody.

A symphony soft, and sweet, and low,
Like the gentlest music the angels know
    In their moments of deepest joy;
'Mid earth's wild clamour thy spirit telling
Of beauty and holiness, upward swelling,
    And mingling with the sky.

A radiant, fadeless Eden flower,
Unfolding in loveliness hour by hour,
    Like a wing-veiled seraph's face;—
Such be the opening year to thee,
Shrouded though all its moments be,
    Unknown as the bounds of space.

Blessings unspoken this year be thine!
Each day in its rainbow flight entwine
    New gems in thy joy-wreathed crown;
May each in the smile of Him be bright,
Who is changeless Love and unfading Light,
Till the glory seem to thy trancèd sight
    As heaven to earth come down.

Bonnie Wee Eric.

BONNIE wee Eric! I have sat beside the evening fire,
And listened to the leaping flame still darting keenly higher,
And all the while a lisping voice and eyes of sunny blue
Out-whispered the flame-whisper, and outshone the flicker too.

Bonnie wee Eric! To his home thoughts pleasantly return,
To long fair evenings in the land of ben and brae and burn;
Sweet northern words, so tunefully upon our Saxon flung,
As if a mountain breeze swept by where fairy bells are hung.

But sweeter than all fairy bells of quaint sweet minstrel tongue,
Rang out wee Eric's gentlest tone when o'er his cot I hung,
And told him in the sunset glow once more the old dear story
Of Him who walked the earth that we might walk with Him in glory.

'He loves the little children so;—does darling Eric love Him?'
I think the angels must have smiled a rainbow-smile above him,
Yet hardly brighter than his own, that lit the answer true,
'Jesus, the kind good Jesus! Me do, oh yes, me do!'

Bonnie wee Eric! How the thought of heaven is full of joy,
And death has not a shadow for the merry healthful boy!
To hear about the happy home he gladly turns away
From picture books, or Noah's ark, or any game of play.

'Mamma, some day me die, and then the angels take me home
To Jesus, and me sing to Him;—Papa and you too come.'
So brightly said! 'But, Eric, would you really *like* to die?'
She answered him; 'then, darling, tell mamma the reason why?'

And then the sunny eyes looked up, and seemed at once to be
Filled with a happy solemn light, like sunrise on the sea;
He said—'Yes, me *would* like to die, *for me know where me going!*'
What saint-like longing, baby lips! and oh! what blessèd knowing!

The lesson of the 'little child' is sweetly learnt from him;
No questioning, no anxious faith all tremulous and dim,
No drowsy love that hardly knows if it be love indeed;
Not 'think' or 'hope,' but—'Oh me *do*,'—'me *know*,'—his simple creed.

Bonnie wee Eric! Hardly launched on this world's troubled sea,
We know the little bark is safe whate'er its course may be,
And short or long, or fair or rough, our hearts are glad in knowing
It will be onward, heavenward still, for he '*knows where he's going.*'

My Sweet Woodruff.

No more the flowers of spring are seen,
And silence fills the summer noon;
The woods have lost the fresh bright green
    Of May and June.

But yesterday I found a flower,
Deep sheltered from the withering rays,
Which might have known the sun and shower
    Of April days.

I did not think again to find
Such tender relic of the spring;
It thrilled such gladness through my mind,
    I needs must sing.

My girlhood's spring has passed for aye,
With many a fairy tint and tone;
The heat and burden of the day
    Are better known.

But by my summer path has sprung
A flower of happy love, as fair
As e'er a subtle fragrance flung
    On spring's clear air.

I hardly thought to feel again
Such dewy freshness in my heart,
And so one little loving strain
    Must upward start.

There was spring-sunshine in my eyes,
I had such joy in finding you
So full of all I love and prize,
    So dear and true.

My heart is richer far to-day
Than when I came a week ago;
How near to me such treasure lay
    I did not know!

The long parenthesis is o'er,
And now, in letters all of light,
The story of our love once more
                We both may write.

I have no words to breathe the praise
Which now for this 'good gift' I owe;
A wordless anthem I must raise,
                But HE will know.

Our Gem Wreath.

HEARD ye the sounds of joyous glee,
And the notes of merry minstrelsy,
And the purling of low, sweet words which start
From the silent depths of a loving heart;
And the gushing laugh, and the rippling song,
As the summer days sped swift along?
        Saw ye the gleam of sunny hair,
And the glancing of forms yet young and fair,
And the dancing light of happy eyes,
And smiles like the rosy morning skies
Saw ye and heard? and would ye not know
What made such mirth and music flow?

There were maidens five, as blithe and free
As the curbless waves of the open sea:
They met;—ye may liken their early greeting
To the dewdrops on a rose-leaf meeting;
Then many a day flew uncounted by,
With Love like an angel hovering nigh,
While the ruby light of his sparkling wing
Flung a tint of joy on everything.
'In books, or works, or healthful play,'
As the merriest lips would often say,
Or in strange attempts to weave a spell
Which might bid the Muses among them dwell,
Or in a stream of mingled song,

Some of their hours have passed along;
Bearing the sound of each pleasant lay,
And the echo of many a laugh, away.
    When the burning day is on the wane,
They wander through some darkening lane,
In quieter converse lingering awhile
'Neath the arching roof of its shadowy aisle.
    Where the latest sunbeams kiss the brow
Of Malvern's Beacon, see them now;
Springing o'er moss-bed, and rock, and stone,
As though the green earth were all their own;
And singing forth to the fair wide scene,
In a loyal chorus, ' *God save the Queen!*'
    Again, from out the busy street,
They pass with gladly reverent feet
Within the old cathedral's shade;
And feel the sacred silence laid
Upon the lips, upon the heart,
By time and place thus 'set apart.'
Then the anthem fills the glorious fane,[1]
Till its solemn tones float back again,
Round arch and column the sound enwreathing,
Till they seem with holy music breathing,—
Music and love; while the choral praise
Images better and holier days.
    Yet once again;—with low bent head,
They are kneeling where the Feast is spread;
Not one is absent, all are there,
Its silent blessedness to share.
Well may a bond of love be felt,
When thus together they have knelt.

Would ye know the maidens five, oh say?
The meek, the merry, the grave, the gay:
Each jewel of all the sunlit cluster
Shines with its own unborrowed lustre;—
Then listen and gaze, while each shall pass,
As a half-seen vision in magic glass.

[1] fane: temple

I.

A quiet summer evening, when the daybeams' heat and glare
Have passed away, and coolness comes upon the cloudless air,
And the soft grey twilight wakes the stars to glisten o'er the hill,
And the only vesper-chime is rung by one low-murmuring rill:

Like such an evening is the soul of that one dark-eyed maid,
Amid earth's restless turmoil like a calm and pleasant shade;
So soothing and so gently sweet her words of deep love fall
Upon the wearied spirit, like the ringdove's forest call.

Well hath she learnt to sympathize with every hope and fear,
Well hath she learnt the sorrowing heart to brighten and to cheer;
Long years of weary weakness have not passed away in vain,
If the holy art of sympathy they taught her to attain.

Her fairy footstep falleth as a noiseless flake of snow,
So violet-like and still that we her presence hardly know;
But like a gleaming vessel-path, far glittering through the night,
She leaves a memory behind of soft and silvery light.

Within the crystal cavern of retirement ye find
That gem of inward radiance, her 'meek and quiet' mind;
Not like the flashing topaz, or the ruby's gorgeous glow,
She is a precious AMETHYST, whose value well we know.

II.

Now turn we to that merry maiden,
With azure eye, and smooth bright hair;
A lily blossom, fragrance-laden,
            Is not more fair.

A dewdrop to the thirsty flower,
A sun-ray gilding every cloud,
A rainbow when the thunder-shower
            Is rushing loud;

A spirit full of pleasant brightness,
That speaks from lip, and cheek, and brow,
To whose glad spell of cheering lightness
            E'en grief must bow.

Her hand hath learnt with wondrous power
Scenes of rare loveliness to trace,
And picture forms with airy dower
   Of beauteous grace.

The breath of flattery hath not tainted
Her simple thought with pride's dark stain:
Because her leaves are richly painted,
   Is the rose vain?

Then, as an orient EMERALD shining,
Long may her loveliness be set
Among the sister-gems, entwining
   Our coronet.

III.

Say, who shall form the vision-centre now?
She of the large, soft eye, and pensive smile,
She of the earnest gaze, and thoughtful brow:
Who would not love to read her looks awhile,
Or list that often silent voice, whose flow
Like distant waterfall is heard, so sweet and low?

Not many summers o'er her youth have cast
Their varying sun and shade, and we might deem
No breath of sadness o'er her soul had passed,
But for that orb subdued, like some lone stream,
Where the sad willows rest in shadowy love,
While its blue depth reflects the sunlit heaven above.

All calmness, yet deep sorrow she hath known,
Dimming the star of hope which shone so clear,
The song of life hath changed its joyous tone,
The pearl of life hath melted to a tear;
But star and song shall rise in brighter day,
And hers that priceless Pearl which none may take away.

Her sorrow, all unspoken, doth but twine
Our earnest love more changelessly around her;
While we look onward, upward, for the time
When Joy's fair garland shall again have crowned her,

Who as the PEARL of all our wreath is gleaming,
In mild and moonlit radiance softly 'mid us beaming.

IV.

Like a flash of meteor light,
Strangely gladdening and bright,
Is the youngest of the band,
Making every heart expand.

Like a petrel on the wave,
What to her though tempests rave?
She will skim each foamy crest,
Making all around her blest.

Like a song-bird of the spring,
She is ever on the wing;
Carolling in blithest glee,
Like the wild breeze, fresh and free.

Like a beautiful gazelle
Bounding over hill and dell;
Like the scented hawthorn-flowers,
Ever scattering blossom-showers.

Can a star of light be found,
Shedding aught but light around?
Joy and gladness must be nigh,
Where her starry pinions fly.

Clear and open as the day,
All may trust her glancing ray,
All must love its rainbow light:
Is she not a DIAMOND bright?

V.

And the last maiden,—what is she?
She sees not herself as others see,
   From an outward point of view;
She only knows the scenes within,
The weary conflict, and the sin,

The strivings a better life to win,
 And the gleams of gladness too.

But little she knows of the secret cells,
Where in lonely twilight the spirit dwells
 In an ever mysterious home,
Where music, and beauty, and sweet perfume,
Grim storms, and the blackness of the tomb,
In morning brightness, and midnight gloom,
 In an untracked labyrinth roam.

How many a chamber within is sealed!
How wondrous the little that is revealed
 In a scarce-caught whispering tone!
Strange thoughts come forth to her outer gaze,
Wild fancies flash with spectral rays,
And feelings glow with uncertain blaze;
 But their fountain is all unknown.

Ah! she would long to glean a ray
From each lovely gem of this summer lay,
 For her own are faint and few.
The tremulous OPAL's changeful light
May emblem her, now dark, now bright,
Yet blending in love with each sister sprite
 In a union fond and true.

————

Such are the five, as now they seem
In the golden haze of Memory's dream.
But the future! who may lift the veil
And read its yet unwritten tale!
The rose, or the thorn, the sun, the cloud,
The gleeful heart, or the spirit bowed,
The song of joy, or the wail of woe,
Which shall be theirs, we may not know.
Then sorrow and joy alike we leave
 In the Hand which doeth all things well,
And calmly from that Hand receive
 All that each coming year may tell.

Our jewel-garland lives by Him;
    We would not ask of Life or Death,
Who first shall break its shining rim;
    It shall be as the Master saith:
He only shall untwine the bond,
So fair and faithful, fresh and fond.
But oh that each who glistens now
    In this verse-woven coronet,
Upon the Saviour's thorn-wreathed brow
    May as a living gem be set!
Then never shall their light grow dim;
Redeemed and sanctified by Him,
Their life and love in blended rays
Shall shine in everlasting praise.

My Name [1]

FROM childish days I never heard
    My own baptismal name;
Too small, too slight, too full of glee
Aught else but 'Little Fan' to be,
The stately 'Frances' not in me
    Could any fitness claim.

Now, in the crowded halls of life,
    May it be mine to bring
Some gentle stir of the heated air,
Some coolness falling fresh and fair,
    Like a passing angel's wing.

My father's name,—oh how I love
    Its else unwonted look!
For his dear sake right dear I hold
Each letter, changed, as he has told,
Long since from early Saxon mould—
    'The rising of the brook.' [2]

---

[1] Suggested by the question, 'What does the letter R in your initials (F. R. H.) represent?'

[2] 'Heavergill'—the heaving or rising of the brook, or gill.

Of music, holiness, and love
    That name will always tell,
While sacred chant and anthem rise,
Or mourners live whose deepest sighs
To echoes of a Father's will
He tuned, or child, or grandchild still
    On his bright memory dwell.

But 'what the R doth represent,'
    I value and revere;
A diamond clasp it seems to be
On golden chains enlinking me
In loyal love to England's hope,
Bulwark 'gainst infidel and Pope,
    The Church I hold so dear.

Three hundred years ago was one
    Who held with stedfast hand
That chalice of the truth of God,
And poured its crystal stream abroad
    Upon the thirsting land.

The moderate, the wise, the calm,
    The learned, brave, and good, [1]
A guardian of the sacred ark,
A burning light in places dark,
For cruel, changeless Rome a mark,
    Our Bishop RIDLEY stood.

The vengeance of that foe nought else
    But fiery doom could still:
Too surely fell the lightning stroke
Upon that noble English oak,
Whose acorn-memory survives
In forest ranks of earnest lives,
    And martyr-souls in will.

---

[1] 'A man beautified with such excellent qualities, so ghostly inspired and godly learned, and now written doubtless in the book of life with the blessed saints of the Almighty, crowned and throned amongst the glorious company of martyrs.'—*Foxe's Acts and Monuments.*

Rome offered life for faith laid down:
    Such ransom paid not he!
'As long as breath is in this frame,
My Lord and Saviour Christ His name
And His known truth I'll not deny:'
He said (and raised his head on high),
    'God's will be done in me.'[1]

He knelt and prayed, and kissed the stake,
    And blessed his Master's name
That he was called His cross to take,
And counted worthy for His sake
    To suffer death and shame.[2]

Though fierce the fire and long the pain,
    The martyr's God was nigh;
Till from that awful underglow
Of torture terrible and slow,
Above the weeping round about,
Once more the powerful voice rang out
    His Saviour's own last cry.

Oh faithful unto death! the crown
    Was shining on thy brow,
Before the ruddy embers paling,
And sobbing after-gusts of wailing
Had died away, and left in silence
That truest shrine of British Islands,
    That spot so sacred now!

In dear old England shineth yet
    The candle lit that day;
Right clear and strong its flames arise,
Undimmed, unchanged, toward the skies,
By God's good grace it never dies,
    A living torch for aye.

---

[1] See Works of Bishop Ridley, Parker Society, pp. 295 and 296.
[2] Ibid.

'Tis said that while he calmly stood
    And waited for the flame,
He gave each trifle that he had,
True relic-treasure, dear and sad,
    To each who cared to claim.
I was not there to ask a share,
But reverently for ever wear
    That noble martyr's *name*.

Faith and Reason.

REASON unstrings the harp to see
    Wherein the music dwells;
Faith pours a Hallelujah song,
    And heavenly rapture swells.
While Reason strives to count the drops
    That lave our narrow strand,
Faith launches o'er the mighty deep,
    To see a better land.

One is the foot that slowly treads
    Where darkling mists enshroud;
The other is the wing that cleaves
    Each heaven-obscuring cloud.
Reason, the eye which sees but that
    On which its glance is cast;
Faith is the thought that blends in one
    The Future and the Past.

In hours of darkness, Reason waits,
    Like those in days of yore,
Who rose not from their night-bound place,
    On dark Egyptian shore.
But Faith more firmly clasps the hand
    Which led her all the day,
And when the wished for morning dawns,
    Is farther on her way.

By Reason's alchemy in vain
　　Is golden treasure planned;
Faith meekly takes a priceless crown,
　　Won by no mortal hand.
While Reason is the labouring oar
　　That smites the wrathful seas,
Faith is the snowy sail spread out
　　To catch the freshening breeze.

Reason, the telescope that scans
　　A universe of light;
But Faith, the angel who may dwell
　　Among those regions bright.
Reason, a lonely towering elm,
　　May fall before the blast;
Faith, like the ivy on the rock,
　　Is safe in clinging fast.

While Reason, like a Levite, waits
　　Where priest and people meet,
Faith, by a ' new and living way,'
　　Hath gained the mercy-seat.
While Reason but returns to tell
　　That this is not our rest,
Faith, like a weary dove, hath sought
　　A gracious Saviour's breast.

Yet both are surely precious gifts
　　From Him who leads us home;
Though in the wilds Himself hath trod
　　A little while we roam.
And, linked within the soul that knows
　　A living, loving Lord,
Faith strikes the key-note, Reason then
　　Fills up the full-toned chord.

Faith is the upward-pointing spire
　　O'er life's great temple springing,
From which the chimes of love float forth
　　Celestially ringing;

While Reason stands below upon
    The consecrated ground,
And, like a mighty buttress, clasps
    The wide foundation round.

Faith is the bride that stands enrobed
    In white and pure array;
Reason, the handmaid who may share
    The gladness of the day.
Faith leads the way, and Reason learns
    To follow in her train;
Till, step by step, the goal is reached
    And death is glorious gain.

Lynton.

WHY does it seem familiar ground?
    I was never here before;
I never saw this fairy dream
Of wood and wave, of rock and stream,
Nor watched the snowy foam-line gleam
    On Devon's bay-loved shore.

It feels as weird and strange as though
    My spirit had been here;
And in the mists of long ago
An outline wavers to and fro,
Now colourless, now all aglow,
    Now faint, now wondrous clear.

I know it now—the tender spell
    On all this pleasant scene;
For memory's first pale flickering light
Falls on a long-forgotten night,
Though conscious lifetime, dark and bright,
    Lies all outstretched between.

The dearest name I ever spoke
    Was on my lips that eve;

We gave her 'welcome home' once more,
Unknown, the last short absence o'er;
And now, she is but 'gone before'
        The palm-branch to receive.

I know it now,—*she* told me all;
        I sat upon her knee,
And heard about the cliff so tall,
The craggy path, the rocky wall,
The ever-chanting waterfall,
        The silver autumn sea:

The steep and dangerous way above,
        The winding dell beneath;
The rushing Lyn, the shadowy trees,
The hills that breast the Channel-breeze,
The white ships bound for western seas;
        One shining marvel-wreath!

A little picture she had brought
        Of Lynton's lovely vale:
I fastened it upon my wall,
Half deeming I had seen it all;
While colours came at fancy's call
        To deck those outlines pale.

Hers then the charm, so strangely sweet,
        Which made me sit and gaze;
'Tis like a breeze from far-off hills,
Or midnight anthem of wild rills,
That cools the fever-fire which fills
        Our hot and hurried days.

It may be that the parting time
        Has more than half gone by,
That ere another twenty years
Have mingled all their smiles and tears,
We may have passed all griefs and fears,
And her dear welcome greet our ears
        To her blest home on high.

Oh, might it be! That far-off land
    Is all unseen as yet:
But when we pass its portals fair,
It may be that some glory there
Sweetly familiar shall appear,
Because we heard it whispered here
By that soft voice, whose accents dear
    We never can forget.

A Birthday Greeting to My Father.

1860

'Tis fully known to ONE, by us yet dimly seen,
    The blessing thou HAST BEEN;
Yet speaks the silent love of many a mourning heart
    The blessing that thou ART;
While traced on coming years, in faith and hope we see,
    'A blessing thou SHALT BE';
Then here in holy labour, there in holier rest,
    BLESSING, thou SHALT BE BLESSED.

A Lull in Life.

'And He said unto them, Come ye yourselves apart into a desert place, and rest awhile: for there were many coming and going, and they had no leisure so much as to eat.'—MARK 6:31.

OH for 'a desert place' with only the Master's smile!
Oh for the 'coming apart' with only His 'rest awhile!'
Many are 'coming and going' with busy and restless feet,
And the soul is hungering now, with 'no leisure so much as to eat.'

Dear is my wealth of love from many and valued friends,
Best of the earthly gifts that a bounteous Father sends;
Pleasant the counsel sweet, and the interchange of thought,
Welcome the twilight hour with musical brightness fraught.

Dear is the work He gives in many a varied way,
Little enough in itself, yet something for every day,—
Something by pen for the distant, by hand or voice for the near,
Whether to soothe or teach, whether to aid or cheer.

Not that I lightly prize the treasure of valued friends,
Not that I turn aside from the work the Master sends,
Yet I have longed for a pause in the rush and whirl of time,
Longed for silence to fall instead of its merriest chime:

Longed for a hush to group the harmonies of thought
Round each melodious strain that the harp of life hath caught,
And time for the fitful breeze Æolian chords to bring,
Waking the music that slept, mute in the tensionless string:

Longed for a calm to let the circles die away
That tremble over the heart, breaking the heavenly ray,
And to leave its wavering mirror true to the Star above,
Brightened and stilled to its depths with the quiet of 'perfect love':

Longed for a sabbath of life, a time of renewing of youth,
For a full-orbed leisure to shine on the fountains of holy truth;
And to fill my chalice anew with its waters fresh and sweet,
While resting in silent love at the Master's glorious feet.

There are songs which only flow in the loneliest shades of night,
There are flowers which cannot grow in a blaze of tropical light,
There are crystals which cannot form till the vessel be cooled and stilled;
Crystal, and flower, and song, given as God hath willed.

There is work which cannot be done in the swell of a hurrying tide,
But my hand is not on the helm to turn my bark aside;
Yet I cast a longing eye on the hidden and waveless pool,
Under the shadowing rock, currentless, clear, and cool.

Well! I will wait in the crowd till He shall call me apart,
Till the silence fall which shall waken the music of mind and heart;
Patiently wait till He give the work of my secret choice,
Blending the song of life with the thrill of the Master's voice.

Adoration.

O MASTER, at Thy feet
  I bow in rapture sweet!
Before me, as in darkening glass,
  Some glorious outlines pass,
Of love, and truth, and holiness, and power;
I own them Thine, O Christ, and bless Thee for this hour.

  O full of truth and grace,
  Smile of Jehovah's face,
O tenderest heart of love untold!
  Who may Thy praise unfold?
Thee, Saviour, Lord of lords and King of kings,
Well may adoring seraphs hymn with veiling wings.

  I have no words to bring
  Worthy of Thee, my King,
And yet one anthem in Thy praise
  I long, I long to raise;
The heart is full, the eye entranced above,
But words all melt away in silent awe and love.

  How can the lip be dumb,
  The hand all still and numb,
When Thee the heart doth see and own
  Her Lord and God alone?
Tune for Thyself the music of my days,
And open Thou my lips that I may show Thy praise.

  Yea, let my whole life be
  One anthem unto Thee,
And let the praise of lip and life
  Outring all sin and strife.
O Jesus, Master! be Thy name supreme
For heaven and earth the one, the grand, the eternal theme.

Adoration.

I

O Master! at thy feet
I bow in rapture sweet!
Before me, as through darkling glass,
Some glorious outlines pass
Of love, and grace, and holiness, and power,
I own them Thine, O Christ, & bless Thee for this hour.

II

O full of truth and grace,
Smile of Jehovah's face,
O tenderest heart of love untold!
Who may thy praise unfold!
Thee, Saviour, Lord of lords & King of kings,
Well may adoring seraphs hymn with veiled wings.

III

I have no words to bring
Worthy of Thee, my King;
And yet one anthem in thy praise
I long, I long to raise;
The heart is full, the eye entranced above,
But words all melt away in silent awe & love.

IV

How can the lip be dumb,
The hand all still and numb,
When Thee the heart doth see & own
Her Lord & God alone!
Tune for thyself the music of my days,
And open Thou my lips, that I may shew thy praise.

Frances Ridley Havergal's fair copy autograph of "Adoration," the last poem in The Ministry of Song. This was found in her Manuscript Book Nº IV. Frances had a specially bound personal copy of her first published volume, The Ministry of Song. This special copy had alternating sheets of printed text and blank sheets, so that across from every right-side page of printed text was a left-side blank page, and turning over the page, every left-side page of printed text faced a right-side blank page. Frances wrote this across from the printed poem "Adoration:" "I began my book with the expression of its devotion to God's glory. I wished to close it with a distinctive ascription of praise to _Jesus_, and therefore without any hesitation at once decided upon placing 'Adoration' where it stands." See pages xiii–xiv of this book.

43

V.

Yea, let my whole life be
One anthem unto Thee,
And let the praise of lip and life
Outring all sin and strife.
O Jesus, Master! be thy name supreme
For heaven & earth the one, the grand, th' eternal theme!

Dec: 31. 1866.

961.

Index to First Lines.